The RTI Daily Planning Book, K–6

Tools and Strategies for Collecting and Assessing Reading Data & Targeted Follow-Up Instruction

Gretchen Owocki

HEINEMANN
Portsmouth, NH

Heinemann
361 Hanover Street
Portsmouth, NH 03801–3912
www.heinemann.com

Offices and agents throughout the world

The author and publisher wish to thank those who have generously given permission to reprint borrowed material:

"Alphabet Chart" from *Literate Days: Reading and Writing with Preschool and Primary Children* by Gretchen Owocki. Copyright © 2007 by Gretchen Owocki. Published by Heinemann. Reprinted by permission of the publisher.

Library of Congress Cataloging-in-Publication Data
Owocki, Gretchen.
    The RTI daily planning book, K–6 : tools and strategies for collecting and assessing reading data and targeted follow-up instruction / Gretchen Owocki.
        p. cm.
    Includes bibliographical references.
    ISBN-13: 978-0-325-01731-0
    ISBN-10: 0-325-01731-X
    1. Reading—Remedial teaching.   2. Reading (Elementary)—Evaluation.   I. Title.
LB1050.5.O96 2010
372.43—dc22   2010000955

Editor: Kate Montgomery
Production: Vicki Kasabian
Cover design: Shawn Girsberger
Cover photograph: © moodboard – Fotolia.com
Typesetter: Kim Arney
Manufacturing: Valerie Cooper

Printed in the United States of America on acid-free paper
14 13 12 11   VP   3 4 5

For David Owocki
and our splendid little Emilia

INSTRUCTIONAL PRACTICES AND TOOLS (CONTINUED)

I wish to express my gratitude to the many people who have influenced the writing of this book:

- The graduate students at Saginaw Valley State University—for their remarkable dedication as thinkers, scholars, and teachers. Their work continually informs mine.

- The kids who have helped with the book—Piper (who has been with me all the way), Michael, Madison, Aurora, Claire, Taylor, and, of course, my dear Emilia.

- Colleagues Melissa Kaczmarek and Kristin Cornelius—for those frequent intellectual encounters that continue to spiral all of us to new planes of understanding.

- Tomek-Eastern teachers Joanne Purzycki and Sandy Munger—for many smart teaching ideas.

- Ruth and Ted Braun and the Saginaw Community Foundation—for supporting faculty scholarship at Saginaw Valley State University, and for making possible the writing of this book.

- My dean, Steve Barbus—for always having wise insight and good humor, and for continually supporting the efforts of his faculty to enrich children's lives through literacy.

- Educators Judy Wallis, David Callejo, and Jeff Williams—for responding thoughtfully and thoroughly to my questions and ideas.

- The staff at Heinemann—for always working to develop new visions, and living up to the highest of publishing standards.

- My editor Kate Montgomery—for big and smart ideas, and for lightening my writing sessions with just the right one-liners. My favorite is about our daughters' initial attempts at swimming: "They really get it about needing air. I like that." Kate, I think you really get it about what authors need. I like that.

Each fall, as the school year begins, you walk into the classroom with a general sense of what you will teach in the area of reading. Because you have knowledge of children, curriculum, and state and national expectations, you have a general sense of what to plan for—and of what your students will learn. If you teach kindergarten or first grade, you plan for students to expand their understandings of the functions of written language; to explore books in engaging ways; and to develop insights into how letters, sounds, words, and text structures work together to make a meaningful message. If you teach older students, you plan for them to experience the bearing of deep comprehension; to expand their experiences with varied types of text; to develop strategies for working with new content and vocabulary; and to develop independence in their reading. Because you know kids and you know curriculum, it is possible for you to do extensive planning before ever meeting your students.

But having a general sense of the kinds of things that children should ultimately be doing in your classroom does not provide you with a starting point for well-tailored teaching. It is only with the assessment of *your* particular students that you begin to gain insight into the particulars of what and how to teach. It is only with *assessment* that you start to identify which students are reading with competence and engagement; which students need intensive support related to decoding or comprehending—and which students might benefit from support beyond what you have planned for the class in general.

When it's at its best, your assessment informs the details and structures of your instruction—and it happens in a continuing cycle. You gather data. You analyze the data to identify your students' strengths and needs. You

Tier 2

Tier 2 instruction is for students who are not making adequate progress in Tier 1—as identified through *universal screening* and *systematic progress monitoring*. (See descriptions of these categories of assessment below. Part 1 contains many tools that may be used or adapted to support the monitoring process.) While RTI legislation does not require a set amount of time, in the primary grades, Tier 2 generally involves an additional 20 to 40 minutes of instruction daily, and usually occurs with a small group. Upper elementary students may need closer to 60 minutes because they are usually further behind and require more catch-up. Tier 2 instruction does not replace Tier 1 instruction but instead offers an additional layer of support.

Tier 2 instruction may be provided by the classroom teacher or a literacy specialist. In the best of circumstances, the school schedule is such that any specialist providing supplementary instruction (whether inside or outside the classroom) is available to offer instruction at times in which regular reading instruction is not taking place. For example, primary grade teachers might schedule reading instruction in the morning, while upper grade teachers schedule it in the afternoon. Supplementary instruction for primary students would then occur in the afternoon with the supplementary instruction for upper grade students occurring in the morning (Shanahan 2008). When instruction is provided by an outside specialist, collaboration with the classroom teacher is essential to maintaining efficiency and consistency.

Regardless of who is providing the Tier 2 instruction, the focus is on supporting and extending Tier 1 instruction—with extra time, intensity, focus, and collaboration aimed at helping the student to be successful with Tier 1. Approximately 10 to 15 percent of students are designated for Tier 2 instruction, with this number varying across schools (Howard 2009; NASDSE 2006).

Tier 3

Tier 3 instruction is generally provided outside the classroom, by a literacy specialist. This additional layer of instruction provides not only more, but also more individualized and/or intensified instruction, than is offered in Tier 2. Again, collaboration between the classroom teacher and specialist is essential, as is high-quality, specific, targeted instruction. Approximately 5 to 10 percent of students are designated for Tier 3 instruction, with this number varying across schools (Howard 2009; NASDSE 2006).

Students who do not show adequate progress with tiered instruction—and the adaptations that result from evaluation of that instruction—are considered for special education. The advantages of the RTI approach versus traditional approaches for referral to special education—and indeed for supporting *all* students in need—are many. Most notably, students in RTI schools don't have to wait for support. If they show a need, they receive supplemental instruction right away, before any referrals are made. The supplemental instruction is connected to what is already happening in the classroom, ensuring coherence and consistency. And the instruction often occurs with peers in the classroom, as an expected part of the classroom day. This brings a sense of normalcy to the notion that some students need extra support.

The success of RTI depends on teachers engaging in thoughtful assessment that leads to thoughtful instruction. But teachers have to be ready—really ready—to take this on. Knowing the competencies to assess, having sound strategies for assessing them, and knowing how to match instruction with demonstrated needs are at the heart of the successful RTI classroom. *The RTI Daily Planning Book, K–6: Tools and Strategies for Collecting and Assessing Reading Data & Targeted Follow-Up Instruction* provides direction and support. The book and Online Resources (see the Companion Resources tab on the book's product page on the Heinemann website to download reproducibles found within the book) provide K–6 teachers, literacy coaches, reading specialists, and school-based teams with (1) a framework for conducting reading assessment; (2) a set of tools for ongoing assessment and tracking of growth; and (3) a set of teaching strategies (small group, intervention group, and whole class) designed to meet student needs as identified through the assessments.

The Three Kinds of Assessment Called for by RTI

Three categories of assessment are generally associated with RTI: *universal screening, progress monitoring,* and *formative observation.* While data from all three categories can be useful in supporting the RTI process, the assessment tools in this book fall largely within the *formative* or instructional decision-making category. The tools are designed to secure specific information for day-to-day decision making and for shaping the details of instruction and intervention.

Before we can delve knowledgeably into the formative tools, it's a good idea to have a sense of what the other categories look like. Understanding the whole picture will help the fundamentals of formative assessment fall into place as they should.

Universal Screening

Universal screening takes place approximately three times per year. A key purpose is to identify students whose reading achievement (or reading-related knowledge) is significantly below what is expected and who therefore might benefit from supplemental instruction. Most schools have a universal screen in place regardless of whether an RTI model is being implemented, as they assess three times per year on competencies that are predictive of performance on state tests (Kovaleski 2009). Many tools and materials are available for universal screening. The National Center on Response to Intervention (www.rti4success.org) provides information on how to use universal screening tools, as well as an evaluation of several professionally published tools. Typically, screening tools are comprised of brief (or relatively brief) assessments that are intended to be strongly predictive of reading achievement. The tools vary in terms of how narrow or broad their predictors are; how accurately they predict which students will actually have difficulty with meaningful reading; and how much information they give teachers to inform daily instruction.

Examples of currently used universal screening tools include Dynamic Indicators of Basic Early Literacy Skills (DIBELS), the Benchmark Assessment System (BAS), the Developmental Reading Assessment (DRA), informal reading inventories, and state reading tests. Regardless of whether your school has already adopted a screening tool, proceed with caution. Some tools have far more useful qualities than others. For example, though DIBELS is quick and easy to administer, it narrowly conceptualizes the act of reading, which tends to narrow curriculum and intervention approaches (Goodman 2006; Pearson 2006). And DIBELS has only "unconvincing" and "partially convincing" evidence when it comes to several aspects of *classification accuracy*, *reliability*, and *validity* (National Center on Response to Intervention), all of which are considered important within an RTI framework.

Universal screening tools do not need to be narrowly focused or quick and easy to administer. Ultimately, they should reflect the literacy performances we most value (Howard 2009). One example of a currently used tool that can provide a broad picture of the reader is the Benchmark Assessment System (BAS) (Fountas and Pinnell 2008). While this assessment is more time-consuming to administer than some of the others (it takes 20 to 30 minutes per student), the benefit is that it provides very useful information for shaping instruction and interventions, including information about fluency, comprehension, phonological awareness, phonics, vocabulary, and text level. Similar tools include informal reading inventories such as the *Qualitative Reading Inventory-4* (Leslie and Caldwell 2005) and the *Analytical Reading Inventory* (Woods and Moe 2007), which assess many of the same competencies as the BAS.

Regardless of the core materials chosen for universal screening, it is important that school teams consider *multiple* sources of evidence as they determine which students should receive supplemental services. Using one source of data is not enough to make such an important decision.

Progress Monitoring

Progress monitoring within an RTI framework involves collecting repeated measures of performance to "(a) estimate rates of improvement, (b) identify students who are not demonstrating adequate progress, and/or (c) compare the efficacy of different forms of instruction to design more effective, individualized instruction" (National Center on Response to Intervention 2009). Progress-monitoring assessments are administered anywhere from weekly to monthly.

Many progress-monitoring tools are available on the professional market, but schools can develop their own. The National Center on Response to Intervention (www.rti4success.org) provides information on how to use progress-monitoring tools, as well as an evaluation of several professionally published tools. As with universal screening tools, some progress-monitoring tools are more effective than others. The monitoring tools your team selects for reading should assess the skills and strategies that have been targeted for intervention; they should show change over time; and they should be sensitive to small changes (Mesmer and Mesmer 2008). It is also important that *oral reading* not be the only measure of performance considered, as some students have oral language difficulties that preclude their ability to show their true levels of proficiency through this medium (German and Newman 2007). And other students, particularly bilingual readers, sometimes read slowly to facilitate comprehension, or become so focused on comprehending that they translate meanings and syntax into their dominant language and end up producing many errors (Goodman, Watson, and Burke 2005). If we do not consider assessments drawn from silent reading, or at least from careful and flexible analysis of oral reading, we run the risk of providing instruction that does not match actual student needs.

Curriculum-Based Measurement (CBM) is often used for progress monitoring. CBM assessments are generally brief and maintain a "steady" rather than an "increasing" difficulty. They result in a quantitative value that can be charted over time. For example, second-grade students might read a second-grade-level passage every four weeks as the teacher documents *words correct per minute* or *percentage of words read correctly*. This form of assessment is intended to produce a "clean" record of growth over time on a skill that is predictive of reading achievement.

An important concept to consider with the use of monitoring tools relates to the fact that they often focus on just one or two skills—and often rely on *time* as part of the measure. While some isolated skills may predict certain components of reading achievement, they do not necessarily predict what overall achievement might look like. For example, strong alphabetic knowledge does not necessarily predict whether a student is (or will become) a strong comprehender. And, considering speed, it is *normal* for the rate of thoughtful reading to ebb and flow, with ebbs occurring especially when the content or features lend themselves to reflection or create a need to stop and think (Flurkey 2006). Related to these concerns, narrow assessment approaches can lead to a narrowing of the instructional focus. For example, if *nonsense word fluency* or *words correct per minute* are the only measures used to monitor progress, an understandable tendency would be to encourage students to focus on decoding and speed over making an effort to construct meaning.

Ultimately, tools that mirror the kind of reading we ultimately want children to engage in are most effective for progress monitoring (Howard 2009; Tierney and Thome 2006). Whatever tools you use, keep in mind that one tool does not make up the whole data set for a teacher. Progress-monitoring data are one indicator that a pattern of progress is acceptable (or not), but one tool cannot identify all of a student's specific needs or the causes for the observed patterns. "A teacher must use other sources of information to determine what actions to take to help students improve . . . diagnostic assessments, informal classroom observations, contacts with home, conferences with school personnel, and other sources for additional information, as necessary, to make decisions about a student's instructional program" (Hasbrouck and Inhot 2007).

Formative Decision Making

Formative reading assessment is at the heart of the daily decision-making process within an RTI classroom. It can take a number of angles, but to fully round out the RTI assessment categories, it must involve gathering the information that is needed (1) to adjust the specifics of teaching to meet individual students' needs and (2) to help students understand what they can do to keep growing as readers.

Formative assessment requires that we observe and interact with students as they read and respond to real text—preferably the types that are used for instruction in the classroom and that ultimately reflect real-world literacies. We document the decoding and comprehending strategies they use, as well as what they have comprehended. We analyze the documentation and use it to plan next steps for instruction. Effective RTI teachers know what to look for in their decoding and comprehension assessments and have a repertoire of strategies for responding with instruction.

It is often the case with formative assessment that we also reach beyond what students do as they are reading real text, in an effort to hone in on specific needs. For example, if a student does not fare well with reading the simplest of texts (say, a one-word-per-page book with supportive illustrations), the teacher may implement an assessment of basic print concepts to determine where, specifically, to take the instruction next. If a student demonstrates a need for picking up a few high-frequency words, the teacher may give a word inventory to determine which words to use for word study. If a student demonstrates low comprehension with nonfiction, the teacher may ask for a think-aloud as the student reads. With formative assessments, we observe and document actual reading as well as implementing specific types of follow-up assessments to hone in on specific areas and concepts that might warrant instruction. We are cautious to not overuse varied forms of assessment, because most often actual reading is what gives us the most valid and useful information about the reader.

With formative assessment, effective teachers don't stop at assessing skills and strategies for decoding and comprehending. They know that a "whole child" is doing the reading and learning, and therefore extend their observations broadly, to aim at understanding the student's interests, attitudes, sources of motivation for reading, text choices, home literacy practices, ways of interacting within groups, situations in which learning seems to best occur, sources of frustration, and so on. Formative assessment includes an examination of the reader with consideration given to the wider context of the child's life.

Contents of the Book and Online Resources

The material in the book is organized into two parts: *Assessment Practices and Tools* (Part 1) and *Instructional Practices and Tools* (Part 2). The Online Resources (see Companion Resources on the Heinemann website) provide a copy of all key reproducibles.

Part 1: Assessment Practices and Tools

Part 1 provides a framework for collecting the types of data that inform responsive instruction and includes a comprehensive set of tools for collecting each type. The material may be used in classrooms regardless of whether an RTI model is in use—but it is particularly useful for teachers and teams working to develop individualized instruction.

The framework guides you to collect data falling into three categories, each representing a *critical factor* affecting reading and its development:

- student backgrounds and characteristics

- text processing

- text comprehending

Teachers need detailed information in each of these categories to provide the most effective instruction possible—detail that goes beyond what universal screening and progress-monitoring tools can offer. It is *only* with such detail that we can provide rich instruction that ensures engaged reading as well as balanced development of the skills and processes of effective reading.

To help you use the data you collect to organize for differentiated instruction, you will find three types of supports: *rubrics*, *data charts*, and *class checklists*. *Rubrics* will help you identify the particular strengths and needs your students demonstrate as they participate in different literacy activities—and the extent of those strengths and needs. You can place students into groups and provide individualized support based on your rubric evaluations. *Class checklists* give an overview of how the entire class is doing on key skills and strategies. These are provided to help you group students for varied instructional experiences and to plan the details of instruction based on your students' demonstrated needs. The *data charts* organize information about children's skills and strategies in a way that gives you a quick overview of growth over time. These are useful for conferences and for individual tracking of progress.

The Online Resources (see product page on Heinemann's website) contain reproducible forms for all of the assessment tools.

Part 2: Instructional Practices and Tools

Part 2 provides a comprehensive set of strategies for teaching and differentiating instruction in each of the three critical factor areas described in Part 1 (*student backgrounds and characteristics, text processing*, and *text comprehending*). The strategies are presented in "if-then" strands that match the assessment categories in Part 1 so that you can use them to address specific needs as they are revealed through the assessments. For example, if you learn through assessment that you have students who are still developing basic print concepts, then you can turn to the print concepts section in Part 2 for strategies to support instruction. If you have students expressing difficulty decoding multisyllabic words, then you can turn to the multisyllabic words section in Part 2 for strategies.

The strategies are coded to indicate whether they are generally used with the whole class, small groups/individuals, or centers/teams. Though a big part of RTI involves creating high-quality small-group instruction, we can't achieve full effect unless the whole day provides enriching literacy experiences.

Enhancing Your Work Within the Tiers

Depending on what you are doing already with your Tier 1 and Tier 2 instruction, the instructional materials in this book can be used as an enhancement, a supplement, or a replacement for some of the existing components.

Many teachers working within an RTI framework have access to a commercial program that guides instruction and/or interventions. Some, either through personal choice or outside influences, adhere rigidly to their scripts, lesson plans, and materials. Yet, research has offered little scientific evidence to support the inflexible use of commercial programs in an intervention design (Allington 2009; Howard 2009). In fact, recent findings on intervention provide evidence for the contrary: "effective patterns of instruction and classroom environments depend on the language, literacy, and self-regulation skills children bring to the classroom and so differ for each student across a continuum" (O'Connor et al. 2009).

Students who demonstrate high needs in the area of reading have a *variety* of profiles. Based on an analysis of students who performed poorly on a statewide assessment, Valencia and Buly (2005) identified six separate patterns of need:

- *Automatic word callers* can decode quickly and with accuracy, but do not read for meaning.

- *Struggling word callers* have difficulty with both word identification and meaning.

- *Slow word callers* decode well, but slowly, and do not read for meaning.

- *Word stumblers* have trouble with word identification but are strong on comprehension.

- *Slow comprehenders* decode accurately and comprehend well, but process text slowly.

- *Disabled readers* experience difficulty with word identification, meaning, and fluency.

Children's needs differ so vastly that a single program designed to support numerous students can only do so much. While commercial programs can provide useful direction regarding ways to organize the curriculum, offer useful resources for teaching, and be in tune with some students' needs, they must be used flexibly. More than anything else, your students need you to use your professional expertise to unravel their needs and to plan instruction that is directly responsive.

Creating High-Quality Small-Group Instruction

While the success of RTI depends on the whole day being enriched with meaningful literacy experiences, it is generally thought that the small-group, individualized instruction (in all tiers) is what will foster the accelerated growth that we want Tier 2 and Tier 3 students to experience. Researchers in the field of reading have identified the following characteristics as strong contributors to effective small-group instruction and intervention. Students are likely to have the best chance of accelerated growth when these small-group practices are in place.

1. *Students engage in meaningful reading for a major portion of the small-group session.* Teachers who are the most effective in supporting children's literacy have been found to devote more time to actual student reading than teachers who are less effective (Allington 2002). While related activities such as word study or building of background knowledge can serve important functions, they should constitute considerably less time during the session than the reading itself. Depending on student needs, in a 30-minute session, they should spend approximately 20 to 25 minutes reading with teacher support. Of course, these practices should be adhered to outside the small-group sessions as well. Students need to read in order to develop and improve their reading.

2. *The reading material used for instruction is engaging and culturally relevant to the participating students.* Research shows a strong connection between engagement and achievement (Braunger and Lewis 2006; Guthrie and Wigfield 2000). "Only when children have a variety of materials available to read and many good personal reasons to want to learn about new ideas and concepts will they read varied genres, write for different purposes, and grow in their ability to use written language effectively" (Goodman 1996a, 224).

    Successful RTI approaches will capitalize on the notion that students who *want* to engage with texts are in the best position to benefit from instruction (Braunger and Lewis 2006). *Engagement* (and more reading) will come as a result of teachers knowing and supporting student interests. An unfortunate fact within the educational system is that we sometimes actually cause *disengagement* by forcing students to read text they find uninteresting and difficult.

3. *The reading material used for instruction is accessible.* Reading develops most easily when the text used for instruction is neither too hard nor too easy; when it is challenging but achievable (Clay 1991; Fountas and Pinnell 2006; Mesmer and Cuming 2009). Compelling research evidence has demonstrated that reading too-hard material produces little or no benefits, yet in many classrooms, *only* grade-level classroom material is used for the instruction of all students (Allington 2009). It is rarely the case in a classroom that

material designated for a particular grade level will be accessible for all students.

When working with English language learners, determining what might be accessible requires a flexible approach. With any given text, English language learners (more than other students) may need support activating background knowledge, understanding key vocabulary terms, or working with complex syntax and semantics. When their entry into the text is mediated appropriately, they can often construct meaning at higher levels than if they had not had initial support (Cappellini 2005). For example, in reading *The Curse of King Tut's Tomb*, a prereading discussion of the terms *mummy*, *tomb*, and *pyramid* might make all the difference in what is comprehended. Or a conversation about potentially confusing syntax might help facilitate meaning. Syntactic structures that often present a challenge include: the verb *to be*, subject-verb-object order, prefixes and suffixes, adjectives preceding nouns, and auxiliary verbs (as in *I can't go*) (Meier 2004). Support with sorting through any possibly confusing structures might make a critical difference in what is comprehended. And when selecting text, it is always important to consider that deepening comprehension in the first language while students are developing the second language can benefit the development of literacy in both languages.

Effective RTI teachers use assessment to identify the types and levels of text with which students can work successfully, and move them along a gradient as they expand their competencies. These teachers understand that the difficulty of the material used may be adjusted up or down depending on the situation. For example, when interest is high or background knowledge is strong, students, including English language learners, may find success with more difficult material. On the other hand, when new strategies are being taught or solidified, easier material may be more appropriate. Effective teachers know that no gradient is perfect for any child. Background knowledge, language knowledge, interest, motivation, and familiarity with particular text features will influence the ease or difficulty of a text for any given child (Clay 1991).

4. *The reading material used beyond the session (for independent reading, partner reading, content reading, homework) offers the opportunity for success.* Students need material they can read across the day—not just during small-group sessions. Usually, offering the

opportunity for success means ensuring that the material is at their independent reading level; a bit easier than the material that is used for instruction. It is with accessible material—and *lots* of experience reading it—that reading processes and content knowledge develop most effectively. Accessible material supports comprehension, fluency development, and consolidation of developing skills and strategies, and it also increases motivation (Allington 2009; Clay 1991; Fountas and Pinnell 2006).

English language learners often need support across the day to make text accessible. In the beginning phases, they access text and construct meaning through nonprint features such as illustrations, graphs, maps, and tables. In the intermediate phase, texts are most accessible when the content is familiar, when the instruction involves making the input comprehensible (such as by referring to illustrations, using visuals, and using gestures), and when the instruction supports children's negotiation of complex structures and abstract concepts. At the advanced level, English language learners are expected to be able to access complex texts with comprehension but may still experience difficulty with complex sentence structures, abstract vocabulary, and low-context concept presentation (Hadaway, Vardell, and Young 2004).

5. *Group sizes are small.* A goal of RTI is that students working in Tiers 2 and 3 will make not only "acceptable" progress, but *accelerated* progress so that they can catch up and work successfully within the peer group. Therefore, the recommended group size is approximately 1:3, as it is "almost impossible" to find a small-group intervention that accelerates growth when more than three students are involved (Allington 2007).

Research comparing the growth of students participating in 1:1 instruction with that of students participating in small-group instruction does not show a significant difference. Therefore, *group* instruction could be considered most practical (What Works Clearinghouse 2009).

6. *Thoughtful assessment is used to plan, differentiate, and revise instruction.* "Thoughtful observation of children takes place in a rich, innovative curriculum in the hands of a knowledgeable teacher who demands and accepts responsibility for curriculum decision making" (Goodman 1996a, 223). The teacher focuses on collecting

a broad range of information within the areas of text processing, text comprehension, and personal factors affecting reading and then differentiates instruction to meet individual student needs. Differentiation can involve varying the amount of time spent with students, the texts and materials used, and/or the types of instructional support and experiences that are provided.

In the interest of differentiation, some students (even in Tier 1) may be scheduled to receive more instructional time than others. Teachers who are most successful in promoting literacy have been observed to spend more time with their students *in need* than with their students who are on target (Allington 2009). While this may raise a question of fairness, the on-target students in such situations have not shown to be at a disadvantage, most probably because the exemplary teacher arranges for their time to be well spent. In the most effective classrooms, teachers provide a *variety* of literacy experiences: exemplary teachers "do not give everyone in the class the same task to do; rather, they individualize assignments. Sometimes this means that students are doing very different things at the same time, sometimes it means they are doing the same thing with adjustments on a student-by-student basis" (Pressley et al. 2001, 221).

7. *Teachers provide explicit instruction and scaffolding focused on the skills and strategies used by effective readers; English language learners receive explicit combined language and literacy instruction.* An explicit approach focuses on the direct teaching of skills and strategies in a way that makes *visible* the processes of effective readers, and is recommended for use with both text processing and text comprehension (Keene and Zimmerman 2007; Villaume and Brabham 2002; Gersten et al. 2008). In general, explicit teaching involves modeling the use of skills and strategies; directly explaining what is being modeled; observing and providing feedback as students try out the skills and strategies; and student self-evaluation.

According to Lenz (2006), different students require different levels of explicitness. Some students independently develop strategies through repeated engagement in reading. Most students are likely to benefit from the teacher providing a direct explanation of the strategy and of how it will support their reading or learning. Some students require explicit description, modeling, and guided practice with feedback for extended periods of time. "Because few instructional materials or programs build in the levels of explicitness or intensiveness required to teach strategies to all students, teachers need to focus their instructional planning and decision making on how to achieve this continuum of instructional intensity" (Lenz 2006, 263). Explicitness works best when it connects significantly with individual learners' actual needs and takes its shape in response to what they are doing as they read. Useful explicitness "involves selecting from all the things one could teach by thinking about the learner. . . . Explicitness, then, is not a feature of the teaching itself, but is a feature of the transaction between teaching, the learner, and the material to be learned" (Bomer 1998, 11–12).

8. *Students engage in talk and social collaboration stemming from their own interests and inquiries.* Talk is a critical part of learning; it is the primary symbol system through which children construct knowledge about the world and extend their thinking beyond themselves. It is through their talk and social experiences that "children grow into the intellectual life of those around them" (Vygotsky 1978, 88).

Research in elementary classrooms shows that exemplary teachers encourage lots of talk, both among children and among children and teachers. High-quality talk is purposeful and connected to curricular topics, but it is conversational rather than characterized by teachers doing all of the asking and evaluating and children doing all the responding (Allington 2002; Braunger and Lewis 2006). High-quality talk generally occurs as children encounter challenging concepts; have control over the direction of their explorations; and read and write about topics they find meaningful (Whitmore et al. 2004).

9. *Communication among members of the decision-making team is ongoing.* Parents, classroom teachers, literacy specialists, special education teachers, speech teachers, and other involved partners work together. The focus is on developing effective instructional practices and working toward a *consistent* structure and approach for those practices. Consistency is critical within tiered instruction, as it lends itself to creating more intensity in the instruction, more coherence, and, importantly, more steady growth (Allington 2007).

To facilitate the communication process among members of the decision-making team, the National Association of State Directors of Special Education (2006) recommends a basic problem-solving method involving the answering of four interrelated questions: (1) What is the problem or issue? (2) Why is it occurring? (3) What are we going to do to address it? (4) Did our intervention work? When focusing on literacy instruction, a team might more specifically frame the questions in the following way:

- What are the student's specific needs as identified through universal screening, progress monitoring, and formative assessments?

- What may be the source of these needs?

- What approach to instruction is warranted? What texts would be most appropriate?

- Is our approach working to create engagement with text? Is it working to create the kind of readers we want our children to become? Is it working to accelerate progress? What evidence shows all of this?

10. *Students work within a classroom community that expects and values differences.* Ironically, a tiered system, with its various forms of assessment and grouping, draws attention to academic differences and therefore runs the risk of convincing some students that they are incompetent, which can ultimately undermine positive achievement. RTI schools must find ways to work against this.

Within a community that learns to *expect* and *value* differences, students come to understand that they all have strengths in some areas of language and literacy and need to work to develop strength in other areas. For example, some kids have well-developed school-based literacies, such as reading stories, searching for information in nonfiction text, and synthesizing and reflecting on academic material. Some students are good with digital literacies—they may have experience with Web browsing, emailing, text messaging, or video games. Some are skilled with functional tasks such as reading grocery lists, recipes, or forms the family must fill out. Everyone has literacies and everyone has literacies to develop.

A "participatory" approach to literacy instruction (Freire 1970; Moll and Greenberg 1990; Wade and Moje 2001) values multiple ways of thinking and knowing and makes use of them in the classroom. For example, within the reading curriculum, rather than using only traditional school-type texts, multiple text types are used to support learning: picture books, reference books, chapter books, textbooks, magazines, comic books, electronic texts, and text related to television, film, visual art, and performance art—all of the texts children might find meaningful in their lives. Text is viewed as a "cultural tool" that shapes what we know as well as how we learn. "The purpose of text use and of learning, then, is to expand the cultural tools to which students have access, not by dismissing or excluding the texts (or tools) they bring to school, but by incorporating them into the curriculum and working with students to make connections among the various texts they explore" (Wade and Moje 2001, np).

If students do not experience such broad perspectives on literacy in school, and if the focus of curriculum and assessment are so narrow that cutoff scores and text levels are all that define students' worth as literate individuals, we can't help but expect that negative self-perceptions, low motivation, and little satisfaction or success with school-based literacies will prevail. Working toward curriculum and assessments that develop well-rounded individuals who are skilled with a wide variety of cultural tools—and that do more than tell children whether they have "achieved" or "failed"—is critical to the success of RTI. Children must feel positive and whole in order to take the kinds of risks that are necessary for developing language and literacy.

1

Assessment Practices and Tools

Getting Started: A Framework for Reading Assessment

Formative reading assessment. Where does it logically begin? To answer this question, it helps to think about what we ultimately want children to be able to do with reading. What is the ultimate goal?

Most teachers agree that we want children to read and comprehend all types of cultural tools (or text types) in a way that meets the purpose at hand. Whether children are reading for pleasure, reading to learn about a topic of interest, or searching for a piece of information, we want them to know how to achieve their specific goals—and at the same time, to feel some enthusiasm for the activity. Therefore, observing students as they engage in real acts of reading, and as they talk about what they read, is at the core of effective assessment. It's where we begin.

It is often the case that initial reading assessments reveal a need to probe further and to differentiate our subsequent assessments. For example, exactly where do we start instruction with the student who skillfully decodes but does not comprehend? Is the issue with comprehension strategies? Attention to text structure? Interest and motivation? Are unfamiliar vocabulary and content getting in the way? Where do we start instruction with the student who has difficulty decoding the easiest text available in the classroom? Does the student have a store of automatically recognized words? Does the student have strategies for decoding unknown words? Are multisyllabic words the problem? What about the student who doesn't *want* to read anything? Where do we start? Differentiating our assessments can help. With the range of knowledge, skills, and backgrounds in any given classroom, different students often require different levels and types of assessments. Therefore, this book contains a leveled tool for the assessment of all K–6 readers—one that involves them in reading real literature over the course of the school year—as well as a set of follow-up tools for diversifying the assessments for individual learners. The assessments may be implemented across tiers, depending on the severity of the student's needs. Formative assessment begins in Tier 1 and extends to Tiers 2 and 3 as appropriate. All tools can be found in the Online Resources (using the Companion Resources tab on the book's product page on the Heinemann website).

Organizing your literacy assessments into three critical factor areas (as outlined in Figure 1–1 and described on the following pages) can lead you to collecting the specific information you need for providing well-rounded instruction and intervention. The three key areas are: (1) student backgrounds and characteristics; (2) text processing; and (3) text comprehending.

Figure 1–1 *Three Critical Areas to Assess for Reading*

Three Critical Areas to Assess for Reading

1. **Student backgrounds and characteristics: Specific concepts to assess**
   - general interests and experiences
   - reading interests and preferences
   - attitudes and self-perceptions about reading
   - nature of engagement in school and home literacy practices
   - language(s) spoken in the home

A major characteristic of effective instruction involves selecting texts that students *can* and *want* to read. Students who have been designated as "struggling" often do not enjoy reading and have low self-concepts as readers. Their motivation is often low. Understanding their interests, backgrounds, and personal characteristics helps teachers to work sensitively with each child and build upon identified strengths.

2. **Text processing: Specific concepts to assess**
   - print concept knowledge
   - letter and sound knowledge
   - phonological awareness
   - word analysis
   - sight word recognition
   - use of graphophonic, syntactic, and semantic cues
   - fluency
   - levels of text that are most useful for instruction and independent reading

Students who are not reading within target ranges need access to "just-right" texts and instruction designed specifically for them. By assessing the various competencies influencing text processing, we can design small-group instruction that stems directly from demonstrated student need and provide reading materials that students can read with success.

3. **Text comprehending: Specific concepts to assess**
   - the meaning constructed
   - the strategies used to comprehend
   - background knowledge that relates to the content being read
   - approach to unfamiliar vocabulary and concepts
   - levels of text that are most useful for instruction and independent reading

Students who are not reading within target ranges need instruction that is focused on meaning making, just as all students do. In recent years, numerous packaged reading instructional programs claiming to be "research based" have emerged on the professional market. Many of these programs isolate phonics and fluency and focus on these alone, yet all readers must learn to negotiate meaning as they process text. Observation aimed at understanding the meaning students construct and how they construct it leads to well-rounded instruction that keeps phonics and fluency *in the service of* comprehension.

Student Backgrounds and Characteristics

Within a strong RTI framework, not only will instruction be planned from a skill and strategy perspective, it will also be planned from a "person" perspective. To teach from a person perspective requires that we delve into finding out about students' interests, their life experiences, and their home language and literacy practices. The emphasis is on getting to know the *person* so that we can meaningfully connect the person with the instruction or intervention. Assessing in the personal domain is as important as assessing any area of reading. When instruction draws on students' personal, social, and cultural know-how, their "experience is legitimated as valid, and classroom practices can build on the familiar. . . ." (Gonzalez 2005, 43). And sociocultural research reveals that "students do not master any school practice without being motivated to enter into it and identify with that practice and without believing that they will be able to function within it and use it now or later in life" (Gee 1999, 362). When students are interested, motivated, and working in contexts they find meaningful, their productive activity is the highest—and it is in this context that they can most ably expand their competencies.

A critical but sometimes forgotten part of assessing in the personal domain involves considering children's personal learning characteristics. Specifically, we want to understand their unique approaches to reading, their attitudes and self-perceptions, and how they respond when faced with challenges and frustrations. The capability and willingness of a student to focus on a task, even when it is a challenge, has shown to contribute to both a sense of academic self-efficacy and to literacy achievement (McTigue, Washburn, and Liew 2009). Unless we pay close attention to personal learning characteristics, it's hard to know how to build on strengths; when to push forward and when to pull back or take another route; and which paths we can take to maintain children's eagerness to reach out for new challenges. Only by knowing the person within can we create environments that will allow *all* children to prosper. "Students can learn. Students usually want to learn, but they must be in a language environment that helps them believe in themselves as learners" (Goodman 1996b, 250). The first set of assessment tools in Part 1 is designed to collect information that aims to help you teach from a person perspective.

Text Processing and Comprehending

Along with background knowledge and personal characteristics, *text processing* and *text comprehending* are the other major factors for focus in reading assessment. While *universal screening* and *progress-monitoring* assessments are often focused on particular skills and are quick to administer, the *formative* assessments that are featured in this book go beyond this, extending deeply into daily reading events and teasing out the specific skills and strategies that need support.

With formative assessments, we evaluate text processing and comprehending *together* because we need to know what the reader is doing to decode print, and *at the same time* to comprehend it. This holds true for all elementary grade readers. When assessing kindergarten and first-grade readers, we are typically very concerned with *text processing*, but focusing on processing alone is not enough. We want even the youngest students to learn to talk about literature and use it as a mechanism for impacting and developing understandings about their worlds—and our assessments in the area of comprehension can lead us to effectively focus our instructional efforts in these areas.

For older students, we tend to place our concerns in the area of *comprehension*, but information about comprehension alone is not enough to provide a full picture of the reader. Sometimes, though students may appear proficient "enough" at comprehending, a more careful assessment of their text processing can reveal some hidden decoding or fluency issues that need to be addressed.

Figure 1–2 illustrates the text processing and comprehending assessment approach that is used in this guidebook. As the figure shows, the central focus is on (1) identifying the student's strengths and needs in *text processing and comprehending* and (2) estimating the *levels and content* that can be read successfully, both independently and with support.

This, *along with information on student backgrounds and personal characteristics*, constitutes the information you need in order to provide effective and well-tailored reading instruction for K–6 students, both within and outside tiered instruction. Part 1 contains a comprehensive set of assessment tools related to each of the critical factors.

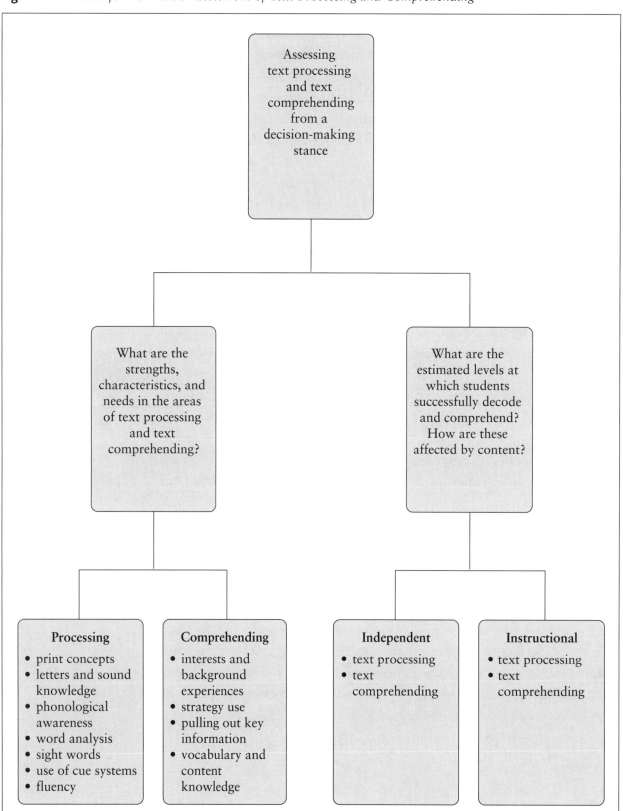

Tools for Assessing Student Backgrounds and Characteristics

The tools in this section are used to assess some of the *background influences and personal characteristics* that affect students' ways of coming to know literacy. Implementing these assessments will provide you with specific information to shape your instruction in both decoding and text processing. The tools should be used early in the school year as you are working to gain broad information about all of your students, and then throughout the year as they are helpful in implementing individualized planning and instruction. The Reader Background and Characteristic Assessment Tools chart lists the reader background and characteristic tools and their uses.

As you select and implement the tools, you might find the Checklist for Self-Evaluation (page 31) to be helpful in ensuring that you are gaining a rounded perspective.

Reader Background and Characteristic Assessment Tools

Type	Tool	Page	Can Be Used to Document the Following	Purpose Within the Tiers
Daily Kidwatching	Kidwatching Notes	33	• Life experiences • Interests • Approaches to learning • Areas of confidence • Situations that cause frustration	• Selecting literature of interest for small groups and independent/partner reading • Generating topics for guided writing • Understanding areas of engagement across the day and using them to inform instruction • Adjusting instruction to ease areas of excess frustration • Understanding how students function in groups across the day and planning to meet their needs in this area
Student Interviews and Surveys	Inventory of Interest and Self-Perception (K–6)	35	• Book preferences • Possible topics of interest for reading • Self-perceptions about reading	• Selecting literature of interest for small groups and independent/partner reading • Generating topics for guided writing • Building relationships with and among students, and fostering a community of understanding and support • Helping students gain metacognitive understandings about their struggles with reading • Understanding how students function in groups across the day and planning to support their work with other students
	Literacy Interview for Young Children (K–2)	37	• Attitude toward reading • Self-perceptions about reading • Areas of reading the student finds challenging • Possible topics of interest for reading	
	Literacy Survey (Grades 2–6)	40	• Attitude toward reading • Self-perceptions about reading • Areas of reading the student finds challenging • Possible topics of interest for reading	
	Interest Survey (Grades K–6)	43	• Student interests • Preferred activities at school • Possible book interests	
	Group Project Survey (Grades 2–6)	46	• Preferences regarding group work • Children the student would prefer working with • Perceptions of difficulties groups have when working together	
	Book Choice Graph	48	• Books of interest in your classroom	

Type	Tool	Page	Can Be Used to Document the Following	Purpose Within the Tiers
Family Collaboration	Survey for Connecting Home and School Learning	52	• Family perceptions regarding the child's characteristics as a reader and student • Student interests • Information about homework/providing support with homework • Information about languages spoken in the child's home(s) • Information about print material in the home • Family perceptions regarding whether the child experiences difficulty with reading	• Selecting literature of interest for small groups and independent/partner reading • Generating topics for guided writing • Using family knowledge to support instruction • Using knowledge about home language and literacy practices to support instruction • Creating meaningful literacy connections between home and school • Setting goals for the student in collaboration with the family • Creating new avenues for family involvement and learning from families
	Tips from the Family	54	• Possible topics of interest for reading • Family perceptions regarding the child's reading performance, and regarding the child's characteristics as a reader and student • Information about homework/support for homework • Goals for the student	
	Family Involvement Questionnaire	56	• Preferred home-school connection activities • Preferred types of classroom involvement • Issues affecting possible involvement	
	Ask the Parent	59	• Books of interest to the student • Home literacy practices • Parent insights regarding the child's experiences in your classroom • Parent insights regarding the child's reading instruction in your classroom	

Type	Tool	Page	Can Be Used to Document the Following	Purpose Within the Tiers
Special Projects	Family Literacy Dig (K–6)	61	• Types of print found in the home • Types of print the student finds meaningful • Specific material the student or family members enjoy reading	• Selecting literature of interest for small groups and independent/partner reading • Generating topics for guided writing • Using home literacy material as a tool for instruction • Using student-generated text as a tool for instruction • Creating meaningful literacy connections between home and school • Creating personal projects that are used for instruction with small groups
	Student Life Maps	62	• Important events in the student's life	
	Student Timelines	63	• Important events in the student's life	
	Read About Me Books	67	• Things student likes • Things student dislikes • Preferred books • Student's family and pets • Highlights of student's life	
	I Am From Poems	68	• Places and people important in the child's life • Important items around home, yard, and neighborhood • Sayings and phrases that are familiar to the student • Important events in the child's life • Meaningful foods • Important smells, sounds, sights, touches	
	Book Talks	69	• Books of interest in your classroom • Reasons students like certain books	
	Oral Histories	70	• Stories from family members and relatives	
	Storytelling	71	• Stories about events in the student's life	

Checklist for Self-Evaluation

Ten Top-Notch RTI Practices:
Background and Learning Characteristics

_____ I have developed a strong sense of the child's interests, both in and out of school.

_____ I have developed a strong sense of the child's attitudes and self-perceptions about reading.

_____ I take note when the student seems frustrated or disengaged, and plan accordingly.

_____ I have inquired into the language and literacy practices used in the home.

_____ I have partnered with the family in a way that allows members to share information about the child.

_____ I have shared information regarding ways family members might observe or become involved with the learning that takes place in the classroom.

_____ I have partnered with the family in collaborative goal setting and decision making regarding the student's learning.

_____ I have ensured that the family is fully informed about RTI and have provided opportunities for discussion and questions.

_____ I value the diverse ways that families support their child's learning, and try to learn about these ways so that I may use them to support my instruction.

_____ I make use of varied cultural tools (text types) in my instruction so that children's home and community literacy practices are of value in the classroom.

Daily Kidwatching Tools

A key way to develop understandings of students' backgrounds and personal learning characteristics is through daily kidwatching. Kidwatching involves informal but knowledgeable observation of the child engaged in various literacy events across the day (Goodman 1996a). Students are observed as they talk, read, write, and interact in groups. During these times, we watch for them to unfold their experiences, interests, and approaches to learning. We need this type of information to provide instruction from a "whole child" perspective.

But far too often we let this important information dissolve within the busy context of the classroom day. While we may remember some basics, we usually haven't documented them well enough to bring them into our planning. All students, especially those who have become disengaged due to many unsuccessful instructional experiences, need to have their personal interests and their lives brought into the classroom to find a solid base for new learning.

Having available a specific clipboard for taking documentation is a good way to begin. Focusing your documentation on one or two key areas can make the process feel doable and can lead to particularly useful data. Possible areas for focus include the following:

- observations about students' general interests and experiences

- times that individual students seem especially engaged or disengaged

- experiences that cause frustration or present a challenge

- how the student participates in and responds to group situations

Page 33 shows a sample observation sheet. You can place one student's name in each box and use the area for note taking. Placing all students' names on just a few sheets ensures that you are documenting for all, and can help you to make a special effort to gain information about children you tend to observe and hear from less frequently than others.

Kidwatching Notes

Student Interviews and Surveys

Another key way to gather background and personal information is through student interviews and surveys. When seeking interview and survey data, it is important to keep in mind that children's personalities and levels of self-awareness have an impact on the ways in which the children reveal themselves to you. For example, when you ask students how they feel about reading or what they enjoy reading, some may tell you what they think you want to hear: "I love reading and I do it all the time! I read everything!" Others will not hesitate to tell you "It's boring," or "I hate it!" Some children may not yet have the language or self-awareness to articulate the specifics of their issues. They may make blanket statements such as, "I don't like reading," yet be unable to define the key reasons that make this statement true, such as "It gives me a headache" or "Every book I try is too hard" or "I haven't found a book that interests me."

Along with complexities of personality and personal awareness, children, influenced by cultural norms, are known to vary widely in their ways of presenting themselves to others. Hence, in line with cultural expectations, some may be hesitant to tout their own competence to you; uncomfortable to draw attention to themselves; unwilling to appear more (or less) knowledgeable or successful than their peers; or ill at ease elaborating for an adult. Many students eligible for RTI services have arrived at a point at which they do not have a sense of agency or self-efficacy when it comes to reading, and they may not be interested in talking about their reading at all.

Triangulating your assessments is a way to ensure that you are seeing the varying "angles" of the child. Triangulation involves using more than one (typically three) data sources to understand the child's competencies and needs. For example, to get to know your students' backgrounds and personal characteristics, you might use ongoing kidwatching, do a written survey with the students, and send home a survey for the family to complete. Pages 35 to 48 provide a set of interviews and surveys to use with children. Page 49 provides an instructional planning form designed to support the integration of student interests throughout the curriculum. Page 50 provides an instructional planning form designed to support teacher attention to student frustrations and perceptions of their reading difficulty. These forms are specifically designed for students receiving tiered instruction and can serve as tools for collaborative planning among the classroom teacher, intervention specialist, and families. Pages 52 to 59 provide a set of resources to use with families and to organize for planning purposes the information you collect. All can be used to personalize the instruction you provide in the areas of text processing and text comprehending.

Inventory of Interest and Self-Perception (K–6)

Name: _____ Date: _____

Look at the display of books your teacher has put at the front of the classroom.

1. If you could read *two* of these books, which would you choose?

Title	Title
Tell why you chose this one.	Tell why you chose this one.

2. What other topics or books should we keep in mind for you?

3. How are you doing with your reading? Tell why.

Inventory of Interest and Self-Perception (K-6)

Name: Aurora _____ Date: 9 / 4 _____

Look at the display of books your teacher has put at the front of the classroom.

1. If you could read *two* of these books which would you choose?

Title	Title
ice mummy	The Snake Scientist
Tell why you chose this one.	**Tell** why you chose this one.
Because, I like to watch discovery chanal and this looks something like it.	I like to learn about animals and this looks interesting.

2. What other topics or books should we keep in mind for you?

I like a magic sort of fantasy kind of book

3. How are you doing with your reading? Tell why.

No, I have a really high lexcile

Literacy Interview for Young Children (K–2)

Name: _____ Date: _____

1. Draw a face that shows how you feel about reading.

2. Are you a good reader?   YES   NO   SOMETIMES

3. What are some things that are hard about reading (even if you think it's easy)?

   _____

   _____

4. Make up two book covers that show what you would like to read about.

Literacy Interview for Young Children (K-2)

Name: CHRIZ   Date:_____

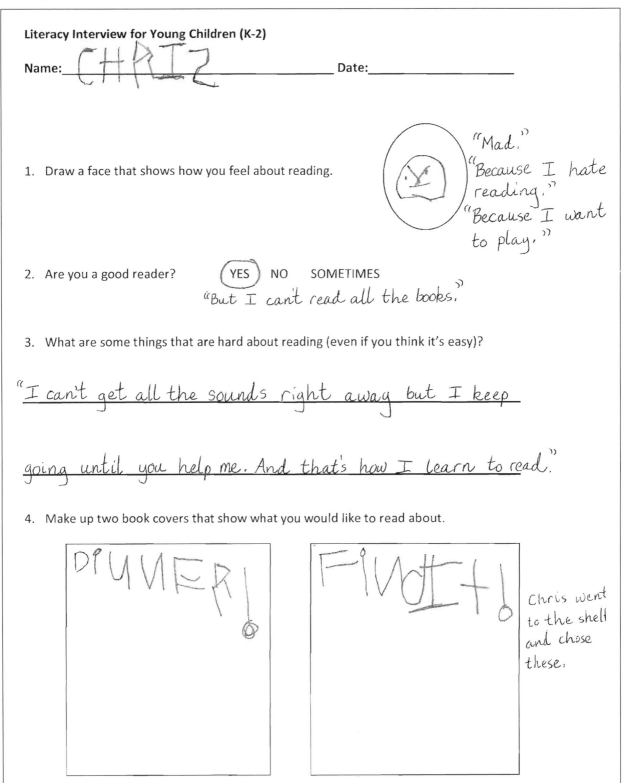

1. Draw a face that shows how you feel about reading.

"Mad."
"Because I hate reading."
"Because I want to play."

2. Are you a good reader?   (YES)   NO   SOMETIMES
   "But I can't read all the books."

3. What are some things that are hard about reading (even if you think it's easy)?

   "I can't get all the sounds right away but I keep going until you help me. And that's how I learn to read."

4. Make up two book covers that show what you would like to read about.

   DIUMERI

   FIVDITI

   Chris went to the shelf and chose these.

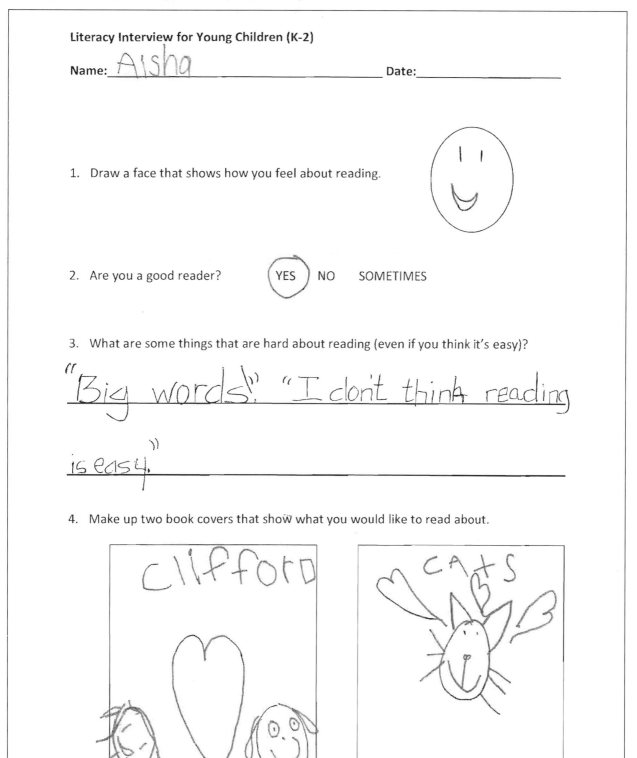

Literacy Interview for Young Children (K-2)

Name: Aisha   Date:

1. Draw a face that shows how you feel about reading.

2. Are you a good reader?   (YES)   NO   SOMETIMES

3. What are some things that are hard about reading (even if you think it's easy)?

    "Big words." "I don't think reading is easy."

4. Make up two book covers that show what you would like to read about.

    clifford

    CATS

Literacy Survey (Grades 2–6)

Name: _____ Date: _____

1. How do you feel about reading?

2. How do you feel about reading out loud? Why?

3. Are there some kinds of reading or writing you are especially good at (such as reading cartoons, reading stories, Web browsing, playing video games, emailing, texting, reading easier texts)?

4. What is hard about reading?

5. Make up two book covers that show what you would like to read about.

Literacy Survey (Grades 2-6)

Name: Taylor _____ Date: _____

1. How do you feel about reading? I love reading

2. How do you feel about reading out loud? Why? I onley like reading out loud to my family. I do not know why.

3. Are there some kinds of reading or writing you are especially good at (such as reading cartoons, reading stories, web-browsing, playing videogames, e-mailing, texting, reading easier texts)?

   All of them

4. What is hard about reading? ~~The long words.~~

   The long ~~words~~ words.

5. Make up two book covers that show what you would like to read about.

Literacy Survey (Grades 2-6)

Name: Mackenzie _____ Date: _____

1. How do you feel about reading?

   Good.

2. How do you feel about reading out loud? Why?

   nerves because I dont want to mess up.

3. Are there some kinds of reading or writing you are especially good at (such as reading cartoons, reading stories, web-browsing, playing videogames, e-mailing, texting, reading easier texts)?

   Reading stories.

4. What is hard about reading?

   Big words

5. Make up two book covers that show what you would like to read about.

Interest Survey (Grades K–6)

Name: _____ Date: _____

What are your favorite things to do at school?

What kinds of things do you like to do outside of school?

Where is your favorite place to go? Tell why.

Do you know of any books you would like to read this year?

Name two things you could write about.

Think of any two things you might like to learn about this year. Write them down.

Interest Survey (Grades K-6)

Name: Claire _____ Date:_____

What are your favorite things to do at school?

Reading and writing.

What kinds of things do you like to do outside of school?

Acting, reading, and danceing

Where is your favorite place to go? Tell why.

My Aunt Sandy's. Because she lives on a lake
and she loves to cook so I'm never hungry.

Do you know of any books you would like to read this year?

Harry Potter and the Half Blood Prince and
book about pets.

Name two things you could write about.

Mystery about missing objets and
adventures.

Think of any two things you might like to learn about this year. Write them down.

Anomils and the History of mishigan.

Interest Survey (Grades K-6)

Name: Madison_____ Date:_____

What are your favorite things to do at school? My favorite things to do at school are S.S, Math, Art, Gym, and L.A.

What kinds of things do you like to do outside of school? I like to play hide n seek tag, riding around, and reading.

Where is your favorite place to go? Tell why. To a family members house because there great to talk to and to play with.

Do you know of any books you would like to read this year? Yes, I would like to read Things Not ~~Heard~~ Heard.

Name two things you could write about. I could right about scary storys and about happy stories that are not so happy.

Think of any two things you might like to learn about this year. Write them down.

In Math I could learn about rounding and in S.S. I could learn about the world.

Group Project Survey (Grades 2–6)

Name: _____ Date: _____

When we do projects and activities, which way works best for you?

- working mostly by myself

- working with one other person

- working with a small group

What can you do to make a group experience work well?

List three students that you would like to work with when we meet in groups.

1.

2.

3.

What problems do your groups sometimes have when they work together?

Group Project Survey (Grades 2-6)

Name: Elizabeth _____ Date: _____

When we do projects and activities, which way works best for you?

- (Working mostly by myself.)

- Working with one other person.

- Working with a small group.

What can you do to make a group experience work well?

Take truns being in charge

List three students that you would like to work with when we meet in groups.

1. Alaire

2. Haley

3. Mackenzie

What problems do your groups sometimes have when they work together?

One porson dosent want to do the assniment

Book Choice Graph

1. Look at the books your teacher has displayed. The names of these books are listed across the bottom of the graph.

2. Write your name in the box above your top book choice.

The Books We Like

	Instructional Planning Form: Planning Small-Group Instruction Based on Student Interests	
Child's Name	Document student interests as observed through kidwatching and interviews/inventories.	Document your plans for the student to read material (independently and with support) that is interesting and accessible.

Survey for Connecting Home and School Learning

Student: _____ Age: _____ Grade: _____

1. How does your child work and play with other children?

   _____

2. How well do you feel your child will work in a classroom setting this year?

   _____

3. How would you describe your child?

   ___ Confident   ___ Easily distracted   ___ Interested in school

   ___ Concentrates well ___ Takes risks   ___ Easily frustrated

   ___ Sensitive   ___ Persistent   ___ Independent

   ___ Talkative   ___ Flexible   ___ Enjoys new social situations

   ___ Dependable   ___ Quiet outside the family ___ Needs lots of encouragement
                                                           to try new things

   Other/Comments: _____

4. What are your child's interests/what does your child enjoy doing?

   _____

5. How does your child respond to homework? _____

6. How much time is available per week for your child to do homework? _____

7. What languages are spoken in your child's home(s)? _____

8. What print material does your child attend to at home (such as newspaper, books, comics, magazines, videos, Internet, games, his/her own writing, or cereal boxes)?

   _____

9. Do you feel your child has any difficulties related to reading or writing? If so, describe.

   _____

Survey for Connecting Home and School Learning

Student: _____Bernadette_____ Age: 6 Grade: 1

1. How does your child work and play with other children?

   Much better than most

2. How well do you feel your child will work in a classroom setting this year?

   I have great expectations

3. How would you describe your child:

✓ Confident	✓ Takes risks	✓ Independent
✓ Concentrates well	✓ Persistent	___ Enjoys new social situations
✓ Sensitive	___ Flexible	
___ Talkative	___ Quiet outside the family	___ Needs lots of encouragement
___ Dependable	___ Interested in school	to try new things
___ Easily distracted	___ Easily frustrated	

   Other/Comments:_____Ø_____

4. What are your child's interests/what does your child enjoy doing? _Also Dance_

   She has broad interests — Swimming and playing w pets.

5. How does your child respond to homework? _When pushed, will do it_

6. How much time is available per week for your child to do homework? _As much as needed_

7. What languages are spoken in your child's home(s)? _Polish, French, English, Spanish_
   none too well!

8. What print material does your child attend to at home (such as newspaper, books, comics, magazines, videos, internet, games, his/her own writing, or cereal boxes).

   All plus some, Internet PBS Kids Stuff.

9. Do you feel your child has any difficulties related to reading or writing? If so, describe.

   x Not aware of Any

Tips from the Family

Student: _____ Age: _____ Grade: _____

1. Suggest three topics/interests your child might enjoy reading about.

   _____

2. How do you feel your child is doing with reading?

   _____

3. How would you describe your child as a reader?

   ____ Confident   ____ Not confident

   ____ Interested   ____ Not interested

   ____ Concentrates well   ____ Easily distracted

   ____ Tries unknown words   ____ Requests help often

   ____ Persistent   ____ Gives up easily

   Other/Comments: _____

4. In which types of classroom situations do you think your child would work well?

   ____ Quieter   ____ Talk-filled

   ____ Highly structured   ____ Less structured

   ____ Activities with specific guidelines   ____ Activities allowing creativity and choice

   ____ Few activity choices   ____ Lots of activity choices

   ____ With one other child   ____ With small groups

   Other/Comments: _____

5. How does your child respond to homework?

   _____

6. Which days and times are good for homework to be accomplished in your home?

   _____

7. What would you like your child to develop/work on this year?

   _____

Tips from the Family

Student: _____Andrej_____ Age: _9_ Grade: _4_

1. Suggest three topics/interests your child might enjoy reading about.

   Space   _Animals_   _Insects_

2. How do you feel your child is doing with reading?

   Expert / HaHa Commensurate w̄ GRADE, I guess?

3. How would you describe your child as a reader?

   _✓_ Confident   ____ Not confident
   ____ Interested   ____ Not interested
   ____ Concentrates well ____ Easily distracted
   _✓_ Tries unknown words ____ Requests help often
   _✓_ Persistent   ____ Gives up easily

   Other/Comments:_____Ø_____

4. In which types of classroom situations do you think your child would work well?

   _✓_ Quieter   ____ Talk-filled
   _✓_ Highly structured   ____ Flexible
   _✓_ Activities with specific   _✓_ Activities allowing creativity and choice
       guidelines
   ____ Few activity choices   _✓_ Lots of activity choices
   ____ With one other child   _✓_ With small groups

   Other/Comments:_____Ø_____

5. How does your child respond to homework?

   Doesnt Like it

6. Which days and times are good for homework to be accomplished in your home?

   Saturday

7. What would you like your child to develop/work on this year?

   Comprehension

Family Involvement Questionnaire

Student: _____ Age: _____ Grade: _____

What sorts of home-school connections do you prefer?

____ visiting the classroom during the school day

____ evening activities or workshops

____ family-oriented homework (reading together, collecting family stories)

____ emails to and from the teacher

____ handwritten notes to and from the teacher

____ phone calls to and from the teacher

____ fall and winter conferences

____ additional conferences to discuss progress and set goals (Please list days and times you

are available either before or after school: _____.)

____ other _____

What knowledge, guidance, or experiences would you like to offer to the classroom?

____ work with children on projects

____ listen to children read

____ bring in a story to read

____ tell a story (personal, family, community, folktale)

____ share a hobby

____ share work-related knowledge

____ share cultural knowledge (traditional stories, ways of living, beliefs)

____ share language knowledge

____ prefer to observe only

____ other _____

Does anything make it difficult for you to participate in school-related activities?

____ conflicts with work

____ younger children at home (or others who may need care)

____ not sure what to do when visiting the classroom

____ not comfortable speaking the language spoken in the classroom

____ transportation

____ other _____

Classwide Preferences for Home-School Connections

Children benefit when their families have varied opportunities to connect with the classroom teacher and school teams. Record the information from the Family Involvement Questionnaire on this form and use it to plan for a variety of types of experiences.

Parent's Name	Visit During the Day	Evening Activities or Workshops	Family-Oriented Homework	Email	Handwritten Notes	Phone Calls	Regularly Scheduled Conferences	Additional Conferences

Classwide Preferences for Involvement in the Classroom

Children benefit when their families have varied opportunities to connect with the classroom teacher and school teams. Record the information from the Family Involvement Questionnaire on this form and use it to plan for a variety of types of experiences.

Parent's Name	Work with Children on Projects	Listen to Children Read	Bring in a Story to Read	Tell a Story	Share a Hobby or Work-Related Knowledge	Share Cultural Knowledge	Share Language Knowledge	Prefer to Observe Only

Ask the Parent

Invite parents to join you in brainstorming effective practices for their child. You may use these possibilities with parents of students working within Tiers 2 and 3, or with all parents.

- **School Literacy Experiences.** Ask parents to spend a few hours in your classroom, observing their child at work and play. Ask how the parents feel the child is faring across the different settings of the day and share ideas for supporting the child's interest, motivation, and positive work habits. Make it a regular practice to ask, "What are you seeing at home?"

- **Reading Instruction Time.** Ask parents to observe their child during your reading instruction time. Share ideas for supporting the child's interest, motivation, and positive work habits.

- **Classroom Book Preferences.** Ask parents to browse through the literature in your classroom and select a few books that might be of interest to their child.

- **Home Literacy Practices.** Ask parents to take a few days to collect examples of the child using reading or writing as part of various activities around the home. The examples could be jotted down in list format. Use the items on the list as a springboard for writing or as a way to gain insight into reading materials that would be of interest to the student.

- **Student Interests.** Ask parents to provide a list of ideas the student may be interested in reading or writing about.

Special Projects

Special projects are another way to develop insights into your students' backgrounds and characteristics as learners. Not only do they serve as a very useful source of data for getting to know your students, they are also a superb way to allow children to draw on their linguistic, social, and cognitive resources to support their literacy learning. Pages 61 to 71 offer ideas for engaging your students in special literacy projects.

Family Literacy Dig

Teacher: Collect ten pieces of print from your home, selecting carefully to represent important aspects of your life (a favorite recipe; a favorite novel; something written by a family member; a package label from a favorite food; instructions for a hobby; something a family member enjoys reading; something connected with a pet; your planner). Show the pieces to your students and talk through their significance. Then, invite the students to bring in a designated number of print items from their own homes (encouraging bilingual students and English language learners to bring in any pieces written in their native or first language) and arrange for two to four students to share each day, preferably with the whole class. Use the experience to get to know your students and to gain an understanding of their home literacy practices.

Follow-up activity: Students make a web that includes information about their pieces of print and use it to write a personal narrative. Or students may choose one item and write a more focused personal narrative.

Student Timelines

On each strip, draw or write an important event from your life. Cut out each strip and staple in an order that makes sense. Make a cover.

Student Timelines

On each strip, draw or write an important event from your life. Cut out each strip and staple in an order that makes sense. Make a cover.

I was born.

We adopted Renji.

We had soccer.

We had presadent Obama.

We visited my cosints.

Student Timelines

On each strip, draw or write an important event from your life. Cut out each strip and staple in an order that makes sense. Make a cover.

Shool

DANS

HealTh

ChRips

PeTs

Read About Me Books

1. Teacher: Create your own *Read About Me* book to use as a model.

2. Arrange for students to make their own books. You may wish to encourage English language learners to write some of the sections in their first language, or in both languages if possible. The following requirements may be used and adapted to meet your students' capabilities.

   • Introduction: Introduce yourself in writing.

   • Family: Include labeled illustrations of important people in your life.

   • Things I like: Use a collage or list to show some things you like.

   • Things I don't like: Use a collage or list to show some things you don't like.

   • Books: List books you've read and enjoyed.

   • Important events from your life: Use a timeline to lay out some important events in your life.

   • Written discussion about your name: Consider telling how you got it; what it means; whether you like it; an interesting story about it; or what you would like to have been named.

   • Autobiographical poem: Include important events from your life.

   • Map of places you have lived or visited.

   • Pets: Include labeled illustrations of important pets in your life.

I Am From Poems (Christensen 2001)

1. Teacher: Write an I Am From poem to introduce yourself to your class. Following are some possibilities to get you started, but do not feel that you need to limit yourself to these starters.

    I am from . . .

    > places
    >
    > foods
    >
    > people
    >
    > items around home, yard, neighborhood
    >
    > sayings or familiar phrases
    >
    > events
    >
    > smells
    >
    > sounds
    >
    > sights
    >
    > touches

2. Provide a list of the "I am from . . ." possibilities (step 1). Allow your students to work in groups to generate personalized lists under as many categories as they would like.

3. Show students how to arrange the items on their lists in aesthetically pleasing ways.

4. Publish the poems as a class book.

Page from Published Class Book of I Am From Poems

> I am from
>   trees, sandboxes, grasses, swing sets, and gardens,
>   pizza and pasta,
>   mom and dad and my friends,
>   "please," "thank you," "good game," "good job," "good try,"
>   "you're doing good."
>
> I am Yvonna.

Book Talks

Set aside a routine time for book talks so that your students can get into a frame of mind to listen to, consider, and enjoy new possibilities. Consider using the time just before independent or partner reading. Book Talks provide an ideal way for students who are not yet faring well with school-based literacies to be successful with a whole-class literacy experience and gain confidence in what they can do.

1. Choose a few of your favorite children's books to talk about, and use them to model what book talks might look like in your classroom. Consider developing a poster-sized planning frame to get children started (see examples). Model how to use the planning frames to develop and present a book talk.

2. Plan enough time for three to five students to talk about a book on any given day. Book talk schedules occur in a variety of formats. For example, three to five students could present two times per week throughout the year, or you could arrange for book talks to occur every day for a week and just do them one week per month.

3. Provide a list of the books the students have chosen to present so that the class can take notes to indicate their favorites. Use the information you collect about preferences to support interest-based independent and small-group reading.

Book Talk Planner (Grades K–1)

> **Book Talk**
> - Show the cover.
> - Name the title and author.
> - Tell whom or what the book is about.
> - Tell why you liked the book. Share pictures or examples.

Book Talk Planner (Grades 2–6)

> **Book Talk**
> - Show the book and tell the title and author.
> - Tell the type of book.
> - Offer a "teaser" that will make others want to read the book. For example, tell about a suspenseful part or provide a glimpse of a conflict without sharing the resolution.
> - Tell who in the class might enjoy the book and explain why.

Oral Histories

Learn about your students and their families through oral history projects.

1. Prepare a note to send home to families. Announce the project and request that families help their child choose an individual to interview (typically a family member).

2. Work with students to develop a list of the kinds of questions that an oral historian might ask. For example:

   - What has been the most important world event in your lifetime?

   - What is your earliest memory?

   - Where did you grow up? Tell me about your childhood homes and neighborhoods.

   - Tell me about your elementary school. What teacher do you remember most? What children do you remember? How did you get to school?

   - What did you play when you were a child? With whom did you play?

   - How did you celebrate holidays or other special days as a child?

   - What stories do you remember hearing your family members tell?

   - What do you remember about your grandparents?

3. Model how to conduct an interview and take notes. To make the project manageable, you might suggest that students (or a subset of students) focus on just two to four of the questions.

4. Show your students ways of transforming the notes into a written document for sharing. They could use their notes to do the following:

   - write a narrative in the first person

   - write a timeline

   - write a biography

   - write one interesting item per page

5. Arrange for students to share their information with the class.

Storytelling

Learn about your students by providing formal opportunities for them to collect and share stories. Storytelling provides a rich context for students to share experiences and learn about the world. It also helps them to develop a sense of story, which enhances their writing and provides a frame for understanding when they are reading.

1. To prepare students for storytelling, model the telling of one or two of your own stories. Focus on real-life experiences.

2. Invite students to plan to tell their own real-life stories. Either assign them to collect a story for homework (families can help and can be encouraged to send in an object to facilitate the storytelling) or organize class time for developing a story in writing.

3. Arrange class time for formal storytelling. If you schedule approximately five students per day, the whole class could tell their stories over the course of a week. If possible, audiotape or videotape the children's stories and make the tapes available for listening or viewing. Allow English language learners to tell their stories in their language of choice.

Tools for Assessing Text Processing and Comprehending

The text processing and comprehending tools include a *reading assessment* and a set of *specific-concept* tools. The Reading Assessment is conducted as students read authentic literature from your classroom. It is designed to help you develop instructional insight regarding your students' decoding and comprehending (for all tiers) and to help you strategically monitor their reading performance and progress. The Reading Assessment is used first among all of the tools because it involves students in the reading of real books. The goal is to see what children do with real texts *first* and base your instruction—and further assessments—on the needs demonstrated in that context. The Reading Assessment offers ways of assessing the following:

- background knowledge for the piece

- phonics knowledge and word analysis

- use of cue systems

- attention to punctuation

- sight word knowledge

- fluency

- comprehension

Note: Effective interventions will not be based on a "little" instruction in each of these areas, or a prescribed amount of each, but on a flexible amount and intensity of each depending on the needs of the learner.

The *specific concept* (follow-up) tools are designed to help you gain additional, and often more specific, insights into your students' text processing and comprehending. After the initial Reading Assessment, it is recommended that you select from the additional tools based on the questions you still have and based on areas in which seeking more detail is warranted. The specific concept tools offer ways of assessing the following:

- print concepts

- letter and sound knowledge

- phonological awareness

- word analysis

- high-frequency word recognition

- use of cue systems

- fluency

- comprehension and use of comprehension strategies

- responses to literature

- content and vocabulary knowledge

The specific use of each text processing and comprehending assessment tool in Part 1 is summarized in the Text Processing and Comprehending Assessment Tools chart (on pp. 74–75). It should be noted that these are not the only tools for reading assessment that you will find in this book. Many of the graphic organizers and other tools for instruction (featured in Part 2) make useful assessment tools as well.

Text Processing and Comprehending Assessment Tools

Type	Tool	Page	Can Be Used to Document and Assess the Following	Purpose Within the Tiers
Text Processing and Comprehending	Reading Assessment	76	• Previewing skills • Phonics knowledge and word analysis strategies and skills • Sight word knowledge • Whether cue systems are being used effectively during the act of reading • Attention to punctuation • Fluency • Whether there is a healthy focus on meaning during the act of reading	• Informing specific, targeted small-group instruction based on needs demonstrated within the context of reading real literature • Determining which areas of text processing and/or text comprehending need to be a focus for instruction • Providing students with appropriately leveled text • Making decisions about moving to more challenging text • Tracking progress across a text gradient
Text Processing—Specific Concepts	Print Concepts Assessment	116	• Concept of letter, sound, and word • Concept of print directionality • Book handling knowledge • Understanding of functions of print vs. illustrations • Concepts of punctuation • Concept that pages of book are connected in meaningful ways	• Informing the specifics of small-group instruction for students needing support with varying aspects of text processing • Determining which areas of text processing need to be a focus for instruction • Tracking progress over time
	Letter and Sound Assessment	119	• Capital and lowercase letter recognition • Knowledge of sounds (phoneme level)	
	Phonological Awareness Assessment	123	• Ability to rhyme, segment, and blend	

	Word Analysis: Features Assessment	125	• General patterns of word knowledge, considering:
			  ◦ Consonants, consonant blends, and digraphs
			  ◦ Vowels
			  ◦ Rimes
			  ◦ Affixes
			  ◦ Multisyllabic words	

	Spelling Inventory	127	• Knowledge of consonant sounds • Knowledge of short vowel sounds • Knowledge of common vowel combinations • Knowledge of consonant blends and doubles • Knowledge of common digraphs • Knowledge of word endings • Knowledge of common rimes	

Type	Tool	Page	Can Be Used to Document and Assess the Following	Purpose Within the Tiers
Text Processing—Specific Concepts	High-Frequency Word Inventory	133	• Automaticity with reading high-frequency words • Word analysis strategies	
	Miscue Documentation and Analysis	137	• Use of cue systems • Word analysis • Attention to punctuation	
	Fluency Assessment	139	• Qualitative dimensions of fluency • Words correct per minute • Quantitative changes in fluency over time	
Text Comprehending—Specific Concepts	Comprehension Strategy and Think-Aloud Observations	144	• Student use of the following comprehension strategies: ○ Monitoring ○ Questioning ○ Making connections ○ Drawing inferences ○ Visualizing ○ Evaluating ○ Determining/summarizing key ideas	• Informing the specifics of small-group instruction for students needing support with varying aspects of comprehending • Determining which areas of comprehending need to be a focus for instruction • Tracking progress over time
	Comprehension After Listening Assessment	148	• How well the student comprehends after listening to a text read aloud (fiction and nonfiction)	
	Fiction Versus Nonfiction Assessment	152	• Whether there is a difference between the student's comprehension of fiction and nonfiction	
	Question Types Assessment	153	• Whether the student answers a variety of question types (lower level and higher level)	
	General Story Map	154	• The student's ability to identify key elements of a story	
	Key Idea Map	157	• The student's ability to identify key information in a text	
	Vocabulary and Conceptual Knowledge Assessment	161	• Whether vocabulary and conceptual knowledge may be the source of comprehension difficulties	
	Vocabulary Knowledge Assessment	162	• Whether vocabulary and conceptual knowledge are supporting or hindering a student's comprehension of a piece	

The Reading Assessment Tool

The Reading Assessment is designed to help you identify your students' text processing and comprehending strengths and needs and monitor their reading progress.

Gathering the Literature

The first step in implementing the Reading Assessment is to gather a set of books to use for assessing. The books you choose are to be set aside and used for assessment purposes only. This will allow you to assess each student with a "cold" read of a new book, to see how the students might do with a new book without your presence.

Figure 1–3 provides a recommended list of books for assessment organized on a gradient from easier to more difficult. The books on the list are leveled according to a widely used benchmark leveling system created by Fountas and Pinnell (2006). This leveling system places books on a scale from A to Z for K–8 readers. Fountas and Pinnell's system is one of the best available because it takes into account more than most leveling systems: most systems rate difficulty using number of words per sentence and number of syllables per word. However, these are not the only kinds of issues that present a challenge for readers and therefore should not be seen as the only criteria that make a text more or less difficult. Fountas and Pinnell's system uses several factors that affect both comprehension and decoding. These are listed in Figure 1–4.

The recommended list of books includes five to six books for each benchmark level (at least one fiction and one nonfiction). The books were chosen based on a variety of features:

- high interest (as demonstrated by children receiving instruction in a university-based literacy center serving approximately one hundred K–8 students per year)
- appealing and supportive illustrations
- representation of varying forms of diversity
- enough substance to determine whether comprehension has occurred
- a structure that lends itself well to retelling

Figure 1–5 shows some examples of the text that appears on the pages of the books on the list so that you can see how the content changes and difficulty increases across the levels.

Figure 1–3 *Recommended List of Books for Assessment*

		Recommended Literature for Assessment		
Grade Level	Book Level	Title	Author	Genre*
K	A	*Can I Have a Pet?*	Hooks, Gwendolyn Hudson	F PB
K	A	*Good Night, Gorilla*	Rathmann, Peggy	F PB
K	A	*I Can Read*	Williams, Rozanne	NF
K	A	*What Do Insects Do?*	Canizares, Susan, and Chanko, Pamela	NF
K	A	*On Our Farm*	Williams, Laura	NF
K–1	B	*My Big Rock*	Perry, Phyllis	F PB
K–1	B	*Cold and Hot*	Sweeney, Jacqueline	F PB
K–1	B	*Bath Time*	Malka, Lucy	F PB
K–1	B	*Monkeys*	Canizares, Susan	NF
K–1	B	*The Things Birds Eat*	Chessen, Betsey	NF
K–1	C	*Where Is My Puppy?*	Hatton, Caroline	F PB
K–1	C	*Cleaning Day*	Figueredo, D. H.	F PB
K–1	C	*Time for Tacos*	Golembe, Carla	NF
K–1	C	*I Eat Leaves*	Vandine, JoAnn	NF
K–1	C	*Fish Print*	Cappelini, Mary	NF
1	D	*I Had a Hippopotamus*	Lee, Hector Viveros	F PB
1	D	*Splat!*	Perez-Mercado, Mary Margaret	F PB
1	D	*Make a Turkey*	Suen, Anastasia	NF
1	D	*Frogs*	Canizares, Susan, and Moreton, Daniel	NF
1	D	*From Egg to Robin*	Canizares, Susan, and Chessen, Betsey	NF
1	E	*The Dashiki*	Taylor, Gaylia	F PB
1	E	*Who Is Coming?*	McKissack, Patricia	F PB
1	E	*Seven Cookies*	Heydenburk, Lorena Iglesias	F PB
1	E	*Bengal Tiger*	Eckart, Edana	NF
1	E	*Gray Wolf*	Eckart, Edana	NF
1	F	*Today I Will Fly!*	Willems, Mo	F PB
1	F	*Ruby's Whistle*	Londner, Renee	F PB
1	F	*Dolphins*	James, Sylvia	NF
1	F	*Manatees*	Rustad, Martha	NF

* F = fiction   NF = nonfiction   PB = picture book   CB = chapter book

Figure 1-3 *Recommended List of Books for Assessment (continued)*

Grade Level	Book Level	Title	Author	Genre*
1	F	*Chinatown Adventure*	Williams, Laura	NF
1	G	*Hondo and Fabian*	McCarty, Peter	F PB
1	G	*Alligator Shoes*	Dorros, Michael	F PB
1	G	*Milk to Ice Cream*	Snyder, Inez	NF
1	G	*Butterflies*	Neye, Emily	NF
1	G	*Giant Pandas*	Freeman, Marcia	NF
1–2	H	*A Little Story About a Big Turnip*	Zunshine, Tatiana	F PB
1–2	H	*The Biggest Snowball Fight!*	Medearis, Angela	F PB
1–2	H	*Crocodile and Hen*	Lexau, Joan	F PB
1–2	H	*Hi! Fly Guy*	Arnold, Tedd	F CB
1–2	H	*What Boo and I Do*	Williams, Laura	NF
1–2	H	*Tale of a Tadpole*	Wallace, Karen	NF
1–2	I	*Emma Kate*	Polacco, Patricia	F PB
1–2	I	*Widget*	McFarland, Lyn Rossiter	F PB
1–2	I	*Surprise Moon*	Hatton, Caroline	F PB
1–2	I	*Froggy Goes to School*	London, Jonathan	F PB
1–2	I	*Tiny Life on Your Body*	Taylor-Butler, Christine	NF
1–2	I	*Truck Trouble*	Royston, Angela	NF
2	J	*Big Mama and Grandma Ghana*	Medearis, Angela Shelf	F PB
2	J	*Owl at Home*	Lobel, Arnold	F PB
2	J	*Henry and Mudge and the Great Grandpas*	Rylant, Cynthia	F CB
2	J	*A Giraffe Calf Grows Up*	Hewett, Joan	NF
2	J	*Fantastic Planet*	Kenah, Katharine	NF
2	J	*Dinosaur Dinners*	Davis, Lee	NF
2	K	*The Good Luck Cat*	Harjo, Joy	F PB
2	K	*Abuela*	Dorros, Arthur	F PB
2	K	*Nate the Great*	Sharmat, Marjorie Weinman	F CB
2	K	*Cheetahs*	St. Pierre, Stephanie	NF
2	K	*Ibis: A True Whale Story*	Himmelman, John	NF
2	K	*Monarch Butterfly*	Gibbons, Gail	NF
2–3	L	*The Lost Lake*	Say, Allen	F PB
2–3	L	*My Buddy*	Osofsky, Audrey	F PB

* F = fiction   NF = nonfiction   PB = picture book   CB = chapter book

Figure 1–3 *Recommended List of Books for Assessment* (continued)

Grade Level	Book Level	Title	Author	Genre*
2–3	L	*Cowgirl Kate and Cocoa*	Lewin, Betsy	F CB
2–3	L	*The Case of the Cool-Itch Kid*	Giff, Patricia Reilly	F CB
2–3	L	*Jaguars*	Squire, Ann	NF
2–3	L	*Oil Spill!*	Berger, Melvin	NF
2–3	M	*Henry's Freedom Box*	Levine, Ellen	F PB
2–3	M	*Marvin Redpost: Kidnapped at Birth?*	Sachar, Louis	F CB
2–3	M	*Solo Girl*	Pinkney, Andrea Davis	F CB
2–3	M	*A Horse Named Seabiscuit*	Dubowski, Mark	NF
2–3	M	*Home to Medicine Mountain*	Santiago, Chiori	NF
2–3	M	*The Story of Chocolate*	Polin, C. J.	NF
3	N	*The Gold Coin*	Ada, Alma Flor	F PB
3	N	*The Year of the Panda*	Schlein, Miriam	F CB
3	N	*Hannah*	Whelan, Gloria	F CB
3	N	*Titanic*	Sherrow, Victoria	NF
3	N	*Saving Samantha*	Van Frankenhuyzen, Robbyn	NF
3	N	*The Milk Makers*	Gibbons, Gail	NF
3–4	O–P	*Indian Shoes*	Smith, Cynthia Leitich	F CB
3–4	O–P	*Stone Fox*	Gardiner, John Reynolds	F CB
3–4	O–P	*Sideways Stories from Wayside School*	Sachar, Louis	F CB
3–4	O–P	*Sequoyah*	Rumford, James	NF
3–4	O–P	*Ice Mummy*	Dubowski, Mark and Cathy	NF
3–4	O–P	*Horse Heroes—Short Story Collection*	Petty, Kate	NF
4	Q–R	*Because of Winn-Dixie*	DiCamillo, Kate	F CB
4	Q–R	*Hatchet*	Paulsen, Gary	F CB
4	Q–R	*The Girl-Son*	Neuberger, Anne	F CB
4	Q–R	*The Story of Muhammad Ali*	Garrett, Leslie	NF
4	Q–R	*Harvesting Hope: The Story of Cesar Chavez*	Krull, Kathleen	NF
4	Q–R	*The Man-Eating Tigers of the Sundarbans*	Montgomery, Sy	NF
4–5	S–T	*Joey Pigza Swallowed the Key*	Gantos, Jack	F CB
4–5	S–T	*The Birchbark House*	Erdrich, Louise	F CB
4–5	S–T	*Taking Sides*	Soto, Gary	F CB
4–5	S–T	*The Great Ships*	Patrick O'Brien	NF

* F = fiction   NF = nonfiction   PB = picture book   CB = chapter book

Figure 1–3 *Recommended List of Books for Assessment* (continued)

Grade Level	Book Level	Title	Author	Genre*
4–5	S–T	*Wolves*	Simon, Seymour	NF
4–5	S–T	*Crazy Cars*	Doeden, Mat	NF
5–6	U–W	*Esperanza Rising*	Ryan, Pam Muñoz	F CB
5–6	U–W	*Wringer*	Spinelli, Jerry	F CB
5–6	U–W	*Around the World in a Hundred Years*	Fritz, Jean	NF
5–6	U–W	*A Boy Called Slow*	Bruchac, Joseph	NF
5–6	U–W	*Buried in Ice*	Beattie, Owen, and Geiger, John	NF
5–6	U–W	*The Tarantula Scientist*	Montgomery, Sy	NF
6	X–Z	*Touching Spirit Bear*	Mikaelson, Ben	F CB
6	X–Z	*Indian Chief*	Freedman, Russell	NF
6	X–Z	*Oh, Rats!*	Marrin, Albert	NF
6	X–Z	*Shutting Out the Sky*	Hopkinson, Deborah	NF
6	X–Z	*Quest for the Tree Kangaroo*	Montgomery, Sy	NF
6	X–Z	*Cowboys of the Wild West*	Freedman, Russell	NF

* F = fiction   NF = nonfiction   PB = picture book   CB = chapter book

Figure 1–4 *Factors Affecting Comprehension and Decoding (Fountas and Pinnell 2006)*

- genre and form
- text structure
- content
- themes and ideas
- language and literary features
- sentence complexity
- vocabulary
- words
- illustrations
- book and print features

User Note: For students who are progressing at expected rates and have many strengths to draw from, incremental changes between (and within) levels are less significant. For a student whose progress is slower, the jumps may offer significant challenges. Therefore, careful kidwatching and attention to variations within and between text levels is important. Keep in mind that all of the features listed in Figure 1–4 may present challenges.

Figure 1–5 *Examples of Leveled Books*

Level	Title, Author, and Example of Text
B	*My Big Rock*, by Phyllis Perry *I play on my big rock.*
E	*The Dashiki*, by Gaylia Taylor *On Sunday, Dad bought a dashiki.* *It had many colors.*
H	*Hi! Fly Guy*, by Tedd Arnold *A fly went flying.* *He was looking for something to eat—* *something tasty,* *something slimy.*
K	*The Good Luck Cat*, by Joy Harjo *I have a cat. a stripedy cat with tickling whiskers and green electric* *eyes. She has the softest fur in the world.*
N	*The Year of the Panda*, by Miriam Schlein *Lu Yi opened his eyes.* *Something was wrong.* *He knew it right away.* *Usually, it was quiet here on the* *farm. The voices of his mother and* *father—of course he knew these. Mr.* *Po, or Ho Yen, or Mrs. Chen, who* *lived on farms close by, he knew* *their voices, too.*
Q–R	*Because of Winn-Dixie*, by Kate DiCamillo *My name is India Opal Buloni, and last* *summer my daddy, the preacher, sent me to the* *store for a box of macaroni-and-cheese, some white* *rice, and two tomatoes and I came back with a dog.* *This is what happened: I walked into the produce* *section of the Winn-Dixie grocery store to pick* *out my two tomatoes and I almost bumped right* *into the store manager. He was standing there all* *red-faced, screaming and waving his arms around.*
U–W	*Esperanza Rising*, by Pam Muñoz Ryan *"Our land is alive, Esperanza," said Papa, tak-* *ing her small hand as they walked through* *the gentle slopes of the vineyard. Leafy* *green vines draped the arbors and the grapes were* *ready to drop. Esperanza was six years old and* *loved to walk with her papa through the winding* *rows, gazing up at him and watching his eyes* *dance with love for the land.*

continues

Figure 1-5 *Examples of Leveled Books* (continued)

Level	Title, Author, and Example of Text
X–Z	*Touching Spirit Bear*, by Ben Mikaelsen *Cole Matthews knelt defiantly in the bow of the aluminum skiff as he faced forward into a cold September wind. Work steel handcuffs bit at his wrists each time the small craft slapped into another wave. Overhead, a gray-matted sky hung like a bad omen. Cole strained at the cuffs even though he had agreed to wear them until he was freed on the island to begin his banishment.*

Doing Your Own Book Leveling

If your school is unable to secure the books on the recommended list, you can use similar books of your own choosing. You will just need to determine an approximate level for these books. Leveling books is relatively simple when you have a set of benchmark books to use for comparison.

1. First, find the levels for a set of books you already have. Scholastic, Booksource, and Bebop have websites that offer leveling information on thousands of books.

    http://teacher.scholastic.com/products/classroombooks/browse_level.asp

    http://bookwizard.scholastic.com

    www.booksource.com

    www.bebopbooks.com

    Note: All of the books on the recommended list can be purchased at these sites.

2. When you have your set of books leveled, you can use them as "benchmarks" to determine the level designations for new books. Be sure to consider all of the factors affecting decoding and comprehension listed in Figure 1–4.

3. As students read the books you have leveled, compare their performance using these books to their performance using the known-level books. Adjust your levels as appropriate.

If you choose your own books for assessment, make an effort to use high-quality literature. More than anything else, we need to know what students can do when they engage with text that contains content worth talking about, thinking through, or investigating further. It is during *engaging* reading events that children are most apt to show us what they know and can do.

User Note: If you use the recommended booklist, you will find *specifically tailored* forms to use for assessment on the website (see pages 106–108 for an example). If you use other literature, a *generic* form can be used for the assessment (see pages 88–95 and Online Resources).

Getting the Right Number of Books

Because the assessment involves a reading-aloud component, you need just one copy of each book. However, you may wish to have several copies of the books you plan to use at each level so that students can continue reading the book after the assessment is complete. While beginners read the whole text during the assessment, more advanced students are asked to just read a segment. You may also want to offer a choice. The more books you have set aside, the more choices you can offer.

As a rule of thumb, try to have the levels listed in Figure 1–6 on hand for assessing, but always with the expectation that some of your students will not be reading within this generally expected range. Ideally, you would collect books three or four benchmark (A–Z) levels below and above the grade level at which you teach.

Administering the Reading Assessment

1. **Determine a starting level.**

   If you have previous assessment data for the student, use it to make your initial book-level selection for the Reading Assessment. (You may find it useful to use the Reading Assessment between more formal assessments required by your school.) If possible, allow the student a choice of texts. If you are assessing in the fall, and the only

Figure 1–6 *Benchmark Levels*

• Kindergarten: A–D	• Fourth grade: O–T
• First grade: B–I	• Fifth grade: S–W
• Second grade: H–M	• Sixth grade: V–Y
• Third grade: L–P	

Based on Fountas and Pinnell's Text Gradient (2006)

data you have are from the previous spring, proceed with caution, as some students fall behind if they have not had access to books over the summer.

If you do not have previous assessment data, begin by making available a range of the recommended books (three or four levels) and asking the student to "Choose one you can read. Not too easy and not too hard."

2. **Pull out the appropriate assessment materials.** You should have available a file that contains copies of the Reading Assessment Form (see pages 88–95) with a Rubric for Fiction or a Rubric for Nonfiction (page 96 or 97) attached to each form. You will need to precopy forms at levels that cover the range of readers in your classroom. The Online Resources contain a tailored form for each book on the recommended list. For the longer books on the list, a portion of the actual text is provided so that it may be used to document and analyze miscues. Your file should also contain the books you will be using for assessment. If you are choosing your own books, preselect the section that will be read and let the student know the stopping point.

User Note: While the Reading Assessment is generally used to assess oral reading in combination with comprehension, it may also be used to assess silent reading in combination with comprehension.

3. **Document the student's text processing and comprehending activity.** Work with the student in a quiet area of the classroom. Use the coding system for documenting miscues (see sidebar) and follow the documentation procedures on the Reading Assessment Forms and Rubrics. Since RTI often depends on teachers collaborating to assess and provide instruction, a standard system for documenting and counting miscues should be developed.

4. **Depending on what you find from assessing with one book, move up or down a level.** The first time you use the tool, go as far as you can to challenge the student. You must find the near-"frustration" level before you can know the highest level at which the student can profitably work. This may require that the student reads more than one passage. After the initial assessment, you will need to move steadily up the gradient, one book at a time. Your goals are to pinpoint patterns of error (this requires that the student read challenging text)

Coding System for Documenting Miscues

If you have a copy of the text to use for documentation, mark miscues on the text. If you do not have a copy of the text, use a check to denote each word that is read correctly. Be sure to document punctuation miscues.

Substitutions: Write the substitution just above the substituted word(s).

Omissions: Cross off the omission, including omissions of punctuation.

Insertions: Write the insertion just above where it occurred, and use a caret to show its placement.

If the reader repeats or self-corrects any section of the text, underline the whole repeated/corrected segment.

Mark corrections with a C.

When tallying miscues, do not count those the student self-corrects.

and to develop insights into how the student is performing within known levels so that you can provide appropriate text for independent and instructional reading.

For students not yet reading books at the A–C level, read aloud a page or two as they follow along—and see if they pick up the pattern. Or you may read the entire book, and then ask that they try again. Observing a young child or a struggling student rereading and patterning a text can be just as useful as observing the cold read. It will show you how the child makes use of text and picture cues and will give you information about whether the text becomes "instructional" after it has been read aloud one time. It is very important that children reading in the A–C level are assessed and instructed as they read real texts, along with instruction focused on letters, sounds, and words. This will help them develop the range of concepts about print that are essential to learning to read.

User Note: The Reading Assessment is not designed to formally determine a student's reading level (though it can be useful in coming to a general estimate). Rather, it is designed to develop qualitative insights into how students perform within known levels so that you can use that insight to inform instruction. Used continually, it can serve as a tool to informally monitor and track growth. See the Estimates of

Independent and Instructional Reading Levels sidebar for information regarding the importance of knowing approximate reading levels.

Estimates of Independent and Instructional Reading Levels

Independent Reading
Knowing your students' approximate text levels for **independent reading** is important. First, too-easy and too-hard books aren't as useful as the "just-right" ones when it comes to developing fluency and comprehension; second, text that is too difficult leads to frustration, low interest, and little reading (Allington 2006). Research has "produced strong, consistent evidence that tasks completed with high rates of success" are linked to greater learning and improved student attitudes (Allington 2001, 44).

Instructional Reading
Knowing your students' highest **instructional reading** level is important as well. You want the text you use for *instruction* to present enough challenge that it can be used to teach meaningful new strategies. The challenge may fall within the realm of vocabulary, content, words, sentences, or generic structures and formats. The key idea is that if we are going to teach something *new*—and to help students develop new strategies—the text should be challenging enough to make that possible.

English Language Learners
Instructional text levels for **English language learners** should be determined with special care. When a text *seems* too difficult, we need to take a close look at the miscues and the retelling to determine whether the text level is *actually* too high. Sometimes, what appears on the surface to be a comprehension problem may be a text that is not well matched to the learner in terms of syntax, vocabulary, content, style of writing, or other such features. Examples of language that may present a challenge are: figurative language, low-frequency words, homophones, homographs, and complex grammar or syntax (Caldwell and Leslie 2009). Before moving to easier text, we should always examine a variety of texts at each reading level and determine whether the level is really too difficult (Cappellini 2005).

5. **Use the assessment data to plan, differentiate, and group students for varying forms of instruction.** The Reading Assessment Forms and Rubrics (pages 88–97) are designed to support these efforts. These materials will help you to identify specific needs in the area of text processing and comprehending and to plan instruction that is based on those needs. These forms also serve as a means for communication among classroom and intervention teachers; they can be used for consistency in collecting data and planning small-group instruction across tiers. The Tracking Form for the Reading Assessment (page 98)

can be used to monitor a student's growth along a text-difficulty gradient. See page 99 for a filled-in example. The example is for third grade. Appendix 2 contains blank forms that may be used for K–6 (they can also be found in the Online Resources). Note that a part of the form is shaded to indicate an "expected" range for growth (based on the work of Fountas and Pinnell), but schools should determine whether these expectations are appropriate in their settings and reshade as appropriate. Page 98 provides a blank form for this purpose. The Grade-Level Growth Chart (page 100) provides a rough estimate of grade-level changes associated with gradient changes (based on Fountas and Pinnell 2008). The Instructional Planning Form (page 101) provides an overview of the needs of the whole class so that ad hoc groups can be formed. The Instructional Planning and Growth-Monitoring Form for Individual Students (page 102) provides a tool for tracking an individual student's needs and growth over time, and page 103 provides a filled-in example.

Reading Assessment Form Levels A–D Fiction

Student: _____ Date: _____

Title: _____ Level: _____

You'll be reading this book. First, preview it and tell me what you notice.

___ title   ___ cover illustration   ___ illustrations   ___ text features   ___ words

What do you know about (name the topic) _____?

Read the title and point to the words. *Document miscues. If student does not read title, read it aloud and then ask student to repeat, pointing to the words.*

After you read, I'll ask you to tell me the important parts. Go ahead and start. *Use a check to document each word read correctly. Document all miscues.*

1:1 correspondence _____   Use of illustrations to support reading _____

When encountering unknown words, student: _____

Words in this passage/book: _____   *Sentences:* _____

What is this story about?

What was a problem (or goal/something the character(s) wanted to do)? What did the character(s) do about it?

Think of something you have experienced like this. Tell about it.

Turn to a page and tell what you think a character was feeling at that point.

Other notes:

Reading Assessment Form Levels A–D Nonfiction

Student: _____   Date: _____

Title: _____   Level: _____

You'll be reading this book. First, preview it and tell me what you notice.

___ title   ___ cover illustration   ___ illustrations   ___ text features   ___ words

What do you know about (name the topic) _____?

Read the title and point to the words. *Document miscues. If student does not read title, read it aloud and then ask student to repeat, pointing to the words.*

After you read, I'll ask you to tell me the important parts. Go ahead and start. *Use a check to document each word read correctly. Document all miscues.*

1:1 correspondence _____   Use of illustrations to support reading _____

When encountering unknown words, student: _____

Words in this passage/book: _____   *Sentences:* _____

What did the author teach about in this book/section?

Tell more about that.

Think of something you have experienced/seen like this. Tell about it.

Why do you think the author wrote this book?

Other notes:

Rubric for Fiction (Attach to Reading Assessment Form)

COMPREHENSION

Element	Level or Content May Be Too Challenging	Good for Instruction	Independent
• Characters • Problem or goal	A critical problem or goal of a key character is not adequately identified. 0–1	Partially describes a critical problem or goal of a key character. 2	Describes most/all relevant aspects of a critical problem or goal of a key character. 3
• Events • Solution	Does not adequately identify key events. 0–1	Accurately retells some key events. 2	Accurately retells key events, including solution/plan for solution. 3
• Prior knowledge • Connections	Demonstrates little prior knowledge; connections show little depth. 0	Demonstrates some prior knowledge; connects on lower levels to ideas or themes in text. 1	Demonstrates prior knowledge; expresses a connection to ideas or themes in text. 2
• Inferences	No demonstrated inferences. 0	Demonstrates some inferring. 1	Demonstrates relevant, insightful inferences that have support in the text. 2

Comprehension score: _____ /10 = _____ %

TEXT PROCESSING

Element	Level or Content May Be Too Challenging	Good for Instruction	Independent
• Accuracy	Below 89%.	90–94%.	95–100%.
• Meaning at sentence level	More than 70% of sentences do not sustain meaning or sound right.	About 70–90% of sentences sustain meaning and sound right as read.	Most sentences sustain meaning and sound right as read.
• Fluency	Little or no expression, phrasing, pacing.	Some expressive, phrased, conversational reading.	Reads expressively, in meaningful phrases, at a conversational pace.

PLANNING: *What needs instruction at this level?*

___ previewing

___ identifying key story elements/ideas

___ topic-related content or vocabulary

___ thinking beyond text/inferring

___ fluency

___ word analysis. List any key parts or features to focus on:

_____

___ sight words. List any key words to focus on:

_____

___ semantic/syntactic miscue quality

Rubric for Nonfiction (Attach to Reading Assessment Form)

COMPREHENSION

Element	Level or Content May Be Too Challenging	Good for Instruction	Independent
• Synthesis	Does not identify main idea. 0–1	Synthesis partially captures overall idea of text. 2	Synthesizes the overall idea of the text. 3
• Determining main/key ideas	Does not identify key aspects of what the author taught. 0–1	Accurately identifies some key aspects of what the author taught. 2	Accurately identifies most/all key aspects of what the author taught. 3
• Prior knowledge • Connections	Demonstrates little prior knowledge; connections show little depth. 0	Demonstrates some prior knowledge; connects on lower levels to ideas in text. 1	Demonstrates prior knowledge; expresses a connection to ideas in text. 2
• Inferences	No demonstrated inferences. 0	Demonstrates some inferring. 1	Demonstrates relevant, insightful inferences that have support in the text. 2

Comprehension score: _____ /10 = _____ %

TEXT PROCESSING

Element	Level or Content May Be Too Challenging	Good for Instruction	Independent
• Accuracy	Below 89%.	90–94%.	95–100%.
• Meaning at sentence level	More than 70% of sentences do not sustain meaning or sound right.	About 70–90% of sentences sustain meaning and sound right as read.	Most sentences sustain meaning and sound right as read.
• Fluency	Little or no expression, phrasing, pacing.	Some expressive, phrased, conversational reading.	Reads expressively, in meaningful phrases, at a conversational pace.

PLANNING: *What needs instruction at this level?*

___ previewing

___ identifying main/key ideas

___ topic-related content or vocabulary

___ thinking beyond text/inferring

___ fluency

___ word analysis. List any key parts or features to focus on:

_____

___ sight words. List any key words to focus on:

_____

___ semantic/syntactic miscue quality

Tracking Form for the Reading Assessment

Student _____ Teacher _____ Grade ____

Initial Assessment Date: _____ Intervention Starting Date (draw line to indicate): _____

Chart the student's highest instructional level. For a level to be designated as highest instructional, the examiner must determine the "too-hard" point, and then move down a level. The student must have a comprehension score of at least 60% *and* an accuracy score of at least 90%.	X–Z																
	U–W																
	S–T																
	Q–R																
	O–P																
	N																
	M																
	L																
	K																
	J																
	I																
	H																
	G																
	F																
	E																
	D																
	C																
	B																
	A																
	Text Levels	Sept		Oct		Nov		Dec		Jan		Feb		Mar		Apr		May

List texts and levels used for the assessment.

Tracking Form for the Reading Assessment: Example

Tracking Form for the Reading Assessment

Student _____ Teacher _____ Grade __3__

Initial Assessment Date: _____ Intervention Starting Date (draw line to indicate): _____

Chart the student's highest instructional level. For a level to be designated as highest instructional, the examiner must determine the "too-hard" point, and then move down a level. The student must have a comprehension score of at least 60% *and* an accuracy score of at least 90%.

Text Levels	Sept	Oct	Nov	Dec	Jan	Feb	Mar	Apr	May
X–Z									
U–W									
S–T									
Q–R									
O–P									
N									O
M								O	
L					O	O	O		
K			O	O					
J	O	O							
I									
H									
G									
F									
E									
D									
C									
B									
A									

List texts and levels used for the assessment.

- Sept: Owl at Home (J); Nate the Great (K)
- Oct: The Good Luck Cat (K)
- Nov: Abuela (K)
- Dec: Cowgirl Kate (L); The Lost Lake (L)
- Jan: My Buddy (L); Home to Medicine . . . (M)
- Feb: Henry's Freedom Box (M)
- Mar: Marvin Redpost (M)
- Apr: Solo Girl (M); The Gold Coin (N)
- May: Hannah (N); Stone Fox (O–P)

Grade-Level Growth Chart

Start Level	End Level	Approximate Grade-Level Growth		Start Level	End Level	Approximate Grade-Level Growth
A	B	0.5		L	M, N	0.5
A	C, D	1.0		L	O	1.0
A	E, F, G	1.5		L	P, Q, R	1.5
A	H, I	2.0		L	S	2.0
A	J, K	2.5		M	N, O	0.5
B	C, D, E	0.5		M	P	1.0
B	F, G, H	1.0		M	Q, R	1.5
B	I, J	1.5		M	S, T	2.0
B	K, L	2.0		N	O, P	0.5
C	D, E, F, G	0.5		N	Q, R	1.0
C	H, I	1.0		N	S, T	1.5
C	J, K	1.5		N	U	2.0
C	L, M	2.0		O	P, Q, R	0.5
D	E, F, G, H	0.5		O	S	1.0
D	I, J	1.0		O	T, U	1.5
D	K, L	1.5		O	V, W	2.0
D	M, N	2.0		P	Q, R, S	0.5
E	F, G, H, I	0.5		P	T	1.0
E	J, K	1.0		P	U, V	1.5
E	L, M	1.5		P	W	2.0
E	N	2.0		Q	R, S, T	0.5
F	G, H, I	0.5		Q	U	1.0
F	J, K, L	1.0		Q	V, W	1.5
F	M	1.5		Q	X	2.0
F	N	2.0		R	S, T, U	0.5
G	H, I, J	0.5		R	V	1.0
G	K, L	1.0		R	W	1.5
G	M, N	1.5		R	X	2.0
G	O	2.0		S	T, U	0.5
H	I, J, K	0.5		S	V	1.0
H	L	1.0		S	W	1.5
H	M	1.5		S	X	2.0
H	O	2.0		T	U, V	0.5
I	J, K	0.5		T	W	1.0
I	L	1.0		T	X	1.5
I	M, N	1.5		T	Y	2.0
I	O, P	2.0		U	V, W	0.5
J	K, L	0.5		U	X	1.0
J	M, N	1.0		U	Y	2.0
J	O, P	1.5		V	W	0.5
J	Q, R	2.0		V	X, Y	1.0
K	L, M	0.5		V	Z	2.0
K	N, O	1.0		W	X	0.5
K	P, Q	1.5		W	Y	1.0
K	R, S	2.0		W	Z	2.0

Instructional Planning Form

What needs instruction before moving to more challenging text? Using the Reading Assessment results, place a check in the appropriate boxes to group students for ad hoc and guided reading instruction.

Child's Name	Level	Previewing	Key Ideas	Thinking Beyond Text	Fluency	Word Analysis	Sight Words	Miscue Quality

Instructional Planning and Growth-Monitoring Form for Individual Students

Student: _____

What needs instruction before moving to more challenging text? Using the Reading Assessment results, place brief notes in the appropriate boxes to plan accordingly.

Level	Previewing	Key Ideas	Thinking Beyond Text	Fluency	Word Analysis	Sight Words	Miscue Quality

Instructional Planning and Growth-Monitoring Form for Individual Students

Student: _____

What needs instruction before moving to more challenging text? Using the Reading Assessment results, place brief notes in the appropriate boxes to plan accordingly.

Level	Previewing	Key Ideas	Thinking Beyond Text	Fluency	Word Analysis	Sight Words	Miscue Quality
J	looked at title only					then where	
K	quickly turned through pages				-rimes (old, one, ope, ose, ost)	what that when then there	
K	quickly turned through pages				-th and wh often con- fused (in writing, too)	thing were what that	
K	thoughtful					through that another	
L					-rimes -ough -ouse	enough thought	
L			not much depth shown (?)		hesitant with multisyllabic words		
L					multisyllabic words		
M			seems focused on literal		much more confident with multisyl- labic words		
M			focused on literal				
M			still focused on literal				

A Test Case

Pages 106 to 113 show an example of a complete Reading Assessment. The student was identified during the third week of school (using a universal screening tool) as one who should receive Tier 2 instruction. The teacher used the Reading Assessment to better understand the student's specific needs.

The first reading is from a section of the book *Owl at Home*, by Arnold Lobel (level J), and the second is from a section of *Nate the Great*, by Marjorie Sharmat (level K). The results from the first reading showed that level J would be "good for instruction." The teacher then tested at level K to determine whether the student would fall within the "good for instruction" range here as well. Finding the highest instructional level allowed her to provide text that was appropriately challenging. The student tested near frustration at level K, making the assessment complete.

Assessing each child in her classroom early in the year, and then spacing out all subsequent assessments over the course of the months that followed, provided a doable pattern for this teacher's assessment. Specifically, it allowed her to do the following:

- **Identify areas of need for special topics instruction.** When ad hoc groups are formed around particular topics, students working within Tiers 2 and 3 can be included for yet another instructional support. After the assessment, the featured student was grouped (ad hoc) for Tier 1 instruction with other students who demonstrated similar strategy needs. She participated in a one-time small-group lesson focused on previewing because she was rather resistant to previewing during the assessment. Students in this group were reading at a wide range of levels but all needed to learn effective strategies for previewing. The student also participated in a series of small-group word study lessons in which each child worked with sight words they had miscued on. Several students had miscued on the same words. (This student worked with *what*, *where*, *there*, *then*, *that*, and *when* because the teacher had noticed some confusion with such words during the assessment.) Finally, the student participated in a series of lessons for students who were just beginning to decode unknown multisyllabic words.

- **Match the student with a text level that would be appropriate for guided reading instruction.** The student was also placed in a group of students (Tier 1) working at the J–K level for instruction. The teacher felt that with instruction, K would be an appropriate level, and J would help to build fluency. This group received instruction while reading several trade books together before being assessed again, and was then regrouped according to the progress the children were making.

- **Match the student with appropriately leveled text for homework and independent reading.** Sending home material at the *independent* level was the goal. The student started by taking home level I and J books, and K books after they had been read with the teacher. The classroom teacher and intervention teacher felt the student should engage in familiar reading and rereading to build her confidence. Research shows that repeated reading improves both fluency and comprehension (Samuels 2002). The student was also encouraged to take home books outside this range if they were of particular interest to her.

- **Inform instruction that occurs throughout tiered intervention.** The intervention teacher and classroom teacher used careful observation from the Reading Assessment to inform the details of their instruction. They continued to use this same assessment tool over the course of the year, focusing their instruction on needs that the classroom teacher had identified on the planning section of the rubrics.

Reading Assessment Form Levels E–Z Fiction

Student: _____   Date: _____

Title: <u>"Strange Bumps" (story in *Owl at Home*)</u>   Level: _____J_____

You'll be reading (part of) this book. First, preview it and tell me what you notice.

_X_ title   _X_ cover illustration   ___ illustrations   ___ text features   ___ words

What do you know about (name the topic) _____?

Read the title and point to the words. *Document miscues. If student does not read title, read it aloud and then ask student to repeat, pointing to the words.*

Scary Bumps? Mysterious Bumps? (Told)

After you read, I'll ask you to tell me the important parts. Go ahead and start. *Use a check to document each word read correctly. Document all miscues.*

Owl was in bed.

"It is time

to blow out the candle

and go to sleep,"

he said with a yawn.

When
Then Owl saw two bumps

under the blanket

at the bottom of his bed.

mysterious
"What can those strange bumps

be?" asked Owl.

Owl lifted up the blanket.

He looked down into the bed.

All he could see was darkness.

go to
Owl tried to sleep,

^

But he could not.

"What if those

mysterious
two strange bumps

grow bigger and bigger

while I am asleep?"

said Owl.

polite
"That would not be pleasant."

Owl moved his right foot

up and down.

The bump on the right

moved up and down.

"One of those bumps

is moving!" said Owl.

Owl moved his left foot

up and down.

The bump on the left

moved up and down.

"The other bump is moving!"

cried Owl.

When encountering unknown words, student: _____

Words in this passage/book: ____138____   *Sentences:* ____16____

What is this story/section about?

About Owl scared of his feet.

What was a problem (or goal/something the character(s) wanted to do)? What did the character(s) do about it?

He's scared of The bumps.
His feet are the bumps.

Think of something you have experienced like this. Tell about it.

When I feel like I don't know where I am in the dark.

Turn to a page and tell what you think a character was feeling at that point.

Owl—nervous because he sees the two bumps under his blanket.

Other notes:

Rubric for Fiction (Attach to Reading Assessment Form)

COMPREHENSION

Element	Level or Content May Be Too Challenging	Good for Instruction	Independent
• Characters • Problem or goal	A critical problem or goal of a key character is not adequately identified. 0–1	Partially describes a critical problem or goal of a key character. 2	Describes most/all relevant aspects of a critical problem or goal of a key character. ③
• Events • Solution	Does not adequately identify key events. 0–1	Accurately retells some key events. 2	Accurately retells key events, including solution/plan for solution. ③
• Prior knowledge • Connections	Demonstrates little prior knowledge; connections show little depth. 0	Demonstrates some prior knowledge; connects on lower levels to ideas or themes in text. 1	Demonstrates prior knowledge; expresses a connection to ideas or themes in text. ②
• Inferences	No demonstrated inferences. 0	Demonstrates some inferring. 1	Demonstrates relevant, insightful inferences that have support in the text. ②

Comprehension score: __10__ /10 = __100__ %

TEXT PROCESSING

Element	Level or Content May Be Too Challenging	Good for Instruction	Independent
• Accuracy	Below 89%.	90–94%.	95–100%. *96%*
• Meaning at sentence level	More than 70% of sentences do not sustain meaning or sound right.	About 70–90% of sentences sustain meaning and sound right as read.	Most sentences sustain meaning and sound right as read. *94%*
• Fluency	Little or no expression, phrasing, pacing.	Some expressive, phrased, conversational reading. *yes*	Reads expressively, in meaningful phrases, at a conversational pace.

PLANNING: *What needs instruction at this level?*

_X_ previewing

___ identifying key story elements/ideas

___ topic-related content or vocabulary

___ thinking beyond text/inferring

___ fluency

___ word analysis. List any key parts or features to focus on:

_____

_X_ sight words. List any key words to focus on:

then

___ semantic/syntactic miscue quality

Reading Assessment Form Levels E–Z Fiction

Student: _____   Date: _____

Title: *Nate the Great* _____   Level: _____K_____

You'll be reading (part of) this book. First, preview it and tell me what you notice.

_X_ title   _X_ cover illustration   ___ illustrations   ___ text features   ___ words

What do you know about (name the topic) _____?

Read the title and point to the words. *Document miscues. If student does not read title, read it aloud and then ask student to repeat, pointing to the words.*

After you read, I'll ask you to tell me the important parts. Go ahead and start. *Use a check to document each word read correctly. Document all miscues.*

My name is Nate the Great.

    d... e...t...e...   *"These words are hard. I hate this book. Scientist? Director?"*
I am a detective.   *Tries sound-by-sound—no blending. TOLD.*

    along
I work alone.

        c...a...s...e...class?
Let me tell you about my last case:

    detective? perfect?
I had just eaten breakfast.

    perfect
It was a good breakfast.

Pancakes, juice, pancakes, milk,

and pancakes.

I like pancakes.

    rung
The telephone rang.

hopped   *d...*   *papers*   *"My goodness I'm stuck.*
I hoped it was a call to look for lost diamonds or pearls   *What does that say?"*
    TOLD.

    molin d-
or a million dollars.

It was Annie.

Annie lives down the street.

 know what   .   papers
I knew that Annie did not have diamonds or pearls
              ^ inserted a period

      mullin dolls
or a million dollars

   lost
to lose.

   last   paper
"I lost a picture," she said.

"Can you help me find it?"

"Of course," I said.

"I have found lost balloons,

   snails
books, slippers, chickens.

     gift
Even a lost goldfish.

   Note
Now I, Nate the Great,

      paper
will find a lost picture."

"Oh, good," Annie said.

"When can you come over?"

"I will be over in five minutes," I said.

"Stay right where you are.

Don't touch anything.

DON'T MOVE!"

When encountering unknown words, student: ____Either goes sound by sound (with no blending) or predicts based on 1st letter____

Words in this passage/book: ___150___   Sentences: ___24___

What is this story/section about?

"It was about a boy who was a detective,"

What was a problem (or goal/something the character(s) wanted to do)? What did the character(s) do about it?

"Well, his friend lost some things. The boy and Annie tried to find it."

Think of something you have experienced like this. Tell about it.

Student looked like she was thinking. Prompted further.
"Not really."

Turn to a page and tell what you think a character was feeling at that point.

"I think Annie was feeling a little sad and worried but the boy was thinking, 'Okay, we can do this!'"

Other notes:

Rubric for Fiction (Attach to Reading Assessment Form)

COMPREHENSION

Element	Level or Content May Be Too Challenging	Good for Instruction	Independent
• Characters • Problem or goal	A critical problem or goal of a key character is not adequately identified. 0–1	Partially describes a critical problem or goal of a key character. 2	Describes most/all relevant aspects of a critical problem or goal of a key character. ③
• Events • Solution	Does not adequately identify key events. 0–1	Accurately retells some key events. ②	Accurately retells key events, including solution/plan for solution. 3
• Prior knowledge • Connections	Demonstrates little prior knowledge; connections show little depth. 0	Demonstrates some prior knowledge; connects on lower levels to ideas or themes in text. ①	Demonstrates prior knowledge; expresses a connection to ideas or themes in text. 2
• Inferences	No demonstrated inferences. 0	Demonstrates some inferring. 1	Demonstrates relevant, insightful inferences that have support in the text. ②

Comprehension score: ___8___ /10 = ___80___ %

TEXT PROCESSING

Element	May Be Too Challenging	Good for Instruction	Independent
• Accuracy	Below 89%. 85%	90–94%.	95–100%.
• Meaning at sentence level	More than 70% of sentences do not sustain meaning or sound right. About 67%	About 70–90% of sentences sustain meaning and sound right as read.	Most sentences sustain meaning and sound right as read.
• Fluency	Little or no expression, phrasing, pacing.	Some expressive, phrased, conversational reading. yes	Reads expressively, in meaningful phrases, at a conversational pace.

PLANNING: *What needs instruction at this level?*

_X_ previewing

___ identifying key story elements/ideas

___ topic-related content or vocabulary

___ thinking beyond text/inferring

___ fluency

_X_ word analysis. List any key parts or features to focus on:
-could focus on -old, -one, -ope, -ose, -ost

___ sight words. List any key words to focus on:
what

___ semantic/syntactic miscue quality

The Specific-Concept Assessments

After administering the Reading Assessment, you may find that you desire more specific information about some of your students' text processing or text comprehending. The *specific-concept assessments* are designed to help you collect this information and to differentiate your assessment practices to better understand particular students. As you consider which of these assessments to use, the guidelines featured in Figure 1–7 may be helpful.

Too often, students not reading within target ranges are perpetually faced with materials that are too difficult. Ultimately, this creates readers who are troubled—and not developing as readily as they could. Differentiating our assessments can help us understand the "depths" of the reader in various areas and tease out how to specifically shape instruction to meet their varying needs. In all cases, it is critical to ensure that students are able to access and make meaning from the material we make available for them to read.

Figure 1–7 *Knowing When to Differentiate and Assess Further*

Information from Reading Assessment	Tools to Gain More Information and Differentiate Your Assessment Practices
The student is not yet reading within the A–C range.	If a student is not yet processing text at the easiest levels (A–C), consider implementing the following assessments: • *Print Concepts Assessment* (p. 116) • *Letter and Sound Assessment* (p. 119) • *Phonological Awareness Assessment* (p. 123) • *High-Frequency Word Inventory* (use words from "first 25" column) (p. 133)
The student demonstrates a need for word analysis strategies.	If a student makes few or ineffective attempts at word analysis, the following assessments will help you to identify the specific types of instruction that are needed: • *Phonological Awareness Assessment.* This will help you understand whether a student understands the process of segmenting and blending word parts. Even older students who express difficulty with analyzing multisyllabic words may have difficulty segmenting words. (p. 123) • *Word Analysis: Features Assessment.* This will help you to determine the strategies the student uses/does not use when attempting to decode an unknown word. It will also help determine which word features the student controls. (p. 125) • *Spelling Inventory.* This will help you to identify the word features the student controls and does not control. You can use this information to guide the words and parts you choose for word study. (p. 127)

Figure 1–7 *Knowing When to Differentiate and Assess Further* (continued)

Information from Reading Assessment	Tools to Gain More Information and Differentiate Your Assessment Practices
The student demonstrates low automatic recognition of high-frequency words.	If a student does not automatically recognize high-frequency words appropriate for the grade level, consider the following: • *High-Frequency Word Inventory.* This will provide information regarding which words to use for word study. (p. 133)
The student demonstrates low fluency.	If a student demonstrates low fluency, you can develop insight into the underlying factors by using the following: • *Miscue Documentation and Analysis.* This will help you to understand the student's use of cue systems, including skill with word analysis. (p. 137) • *Qualitative Dimensions of Fluency Rubric.* This will provide information regarding the specific qualitative aspects of fluency that may be causing an issue. (p. 141) • *Quantitative Dimensions of Fluency Scale.* This will provide information regarding the student's accuracy and speed in relation to general grade-level expectations for fluency. (p. 142)
The student demonstrates low comprehension.	If a student demonstrates low comprehension, consider the following: • *Comprehension Strategy Observations.* This will help you probe into your students' daily use of comprehension strategies, which can be observed as they read, discuss, and respond to different texts in different situations. (p. 144) • *Comprehension After Listening Assessment.* This will help to determine whether the student can listen to and understand grade-level text when decoding is removed from the experience. (p. 148) • *Fiction Versus Nonfiction Assessment.* This will help you determine whether there is a general difference in comprehension with fiction versus nonfiction. (p. 152) • *Question Types Assessment.* This will help you determine whether the student answers both literal and higher-level questions. (p. 153) • *General Story Map with Rubric.* This tool can be used to determine whether the student can identify and write about (or draw) the key elements of a story. (p. 154) • *Key Ideas Map with Rubric.* This tool can be used to determine whether the student can identify and write about (or draw) a key idea from a nonfiction text. (p. 157) • *Vocabulary and Conceptual Knowledge Assessment.* This will help you determine whether the student needs support with comprehension strategies, with vocabulary, or both. (p. 161) • *Vocabulary Knowledge Assessment.* This will help you to determine a student's level of familiarity with words in the text before he or she reads. (p. 162)

Print Concepts Assessment

The Print Concepts Assessment (based on the early works of Marie Clay and Yetta Goodman) is typically implemented with preschool and kindergarten students—especially when there is a question about the amount of experience children have had with books and the nature of their book-handling skills. Students who do not read texts at the A–C level should be assessed with this tool. The Print Concept Assessment may be administered in a one-to-one setting or with a small group. Part 2 contains a strand of instructional practices for students needing support developing print concept knowledge.

Print Concepts Assessment

Name: _____ Date: _____

Hand the student a book. Pose the following questions/prompts and document the child's response.

Question/Prompt	Notes
Show me the front of the book.	
Where is the title?	
Show me where the story begins.	
Show me where you read first. Use your finger to show me how you read. Where do you go next?	
Show me a letter.	
Show me a word. What sound does it begin with?	
Show me the word _____. (Choose a few frequently used words.)	
Show me a period. What is it for? Show me a question mark. What is it for?	
Now you follow with your finger as I read. (Read a few pages.) What do you think will happen next? (Finish reading the text to the student.)	
What was this about?	

Print Concepts Assessment

Name: _Kyle_   Date: _9 - 14_

Hand the student a book. Pose the following questions/prompts and document the child's response.

Question/Prompt	Notes
Show me the front of the book.	✓
Where is the title?	"What's that?"
Show me where the story begins.	✓ Skips over front matter and points to picture on first page.
Show me where you read first. Use your finger to show me how you read. Where do you go next?	Points to print but moves finger in a circular motion
Show me a letter.	✓
Show me a word. What sound does it begin with?	Points to a letter. Doesn't name the letter or sound.
Show me the word _____. (Choose a few frequently used words).	—
Show me a period. What is it for? Show me a question mark. What is it for?	—
Now you follow with your finger as I read. (Read a few pages). What do you think will happen next? (Finish reading the text to the student.)	Circular motion
What was this about?	✓ "a girl and dad cleaning up the house"

Letter and Sound Assessment

The *Letter and Sound Assessment* is typically administered with preschool, kindergarten, and first grade students. By first grade, many students recognize most or all letters of the alphabet, and some are reading well enough that their knowledge of basic letter-sound relationships need not be a focus for assessment. By making it a practice to assess actual reading first (use the Reading Assessment tool), we can determine whether isolated letter or letter-sound assessments are warranted. Informal observations of children's writing also provide useful information about letter and sound knowledge, and may preclude the need to administer the more formal letters and sounds assessment. Part 2 contains a strand of instructional practices for students needing support developing letter and sound knowledge.

Letter and Sound Assessment: Teacher Form

Student Name: _____

Uncover one row at a time on the Student Form as the student names all of the capital and lowercase letters. Then, use the capital letter set to ask the sound that each letter makes. Highlight correct responses, using a different color each time the form is used. For each incorrect response, document what the student says.

Capital Letters

D	J	Z	E
W	P	I	X
V	O	H	C
U	N	G	Y
T	M	F	A
S	L	B	Q
R	K	Date: _____ Correct: _____/26	
		Date: _____ Correct: _____/26	
		Date: _____ Correct: _____/26	
		Date: _____ Correct: _____/26	

Lowercase Letters

d	j	z	e
w	p	i	x
v	o	h	c
u	n	g	y
t	m	f	a
s	l	b	q
r	k	Date: _____ Correct: _____/26	
		Date: _____ Correct: _____/26	
		Date: _____ Correct: _____/26	
		Date: _____ Correct: _____/26	

Isolated Sounds

D	J	Z	E
W	P	I	X
V	O	H	C
U	N	G	Y
T	M	F	A
S	L	B	Q
R	K	Date: _____ Correct: _____/26	
		Date: _____ Correct: _____/26	
		Date: _____ Correct: _____/26	
		Date: _____ Correct: _____/26	

Letter and Sound Assessment: Student Form

D	J	Z	E
W	P	I	X
V	O	H	C
U	N	G	Y
T	M	F	A
S	L	B	Q
R	K		

d	j	z	e
w	p	i	x
v	o	h	c
u	n	g	y
t	m	f	a
s	l	b	q
r	k		

Letter and Sound Assessment: Class Chart

Date: _____

After the assessment, place a check by each known uppercase letter and lowercase letter. Record the number of known sounds at the bottom. Use the results to track growth and group for instruction.

List Children's Names	u	l	u	l	u	l	u	l	u	l	u	l	u	l	u	l	u	l	u	l	u	l	u	l	u	l	u	l	u	l
Aa																														
Bb																														
Cc																														
Dd																														
Ed																														
Ff																														
Gg																														
Hh																														
Ii																														
Jj																														
Kk																														
Ll																														
Mm																														
Nn																														
Oo																														
Pp																														
Qq																														
Rr																														
Ss																														
Tt																														
Uu																														
Vv																														
Ww																														
Xx																														
Yy																														
Zz																														
Total known letters																														
Total known sounds																														

Phonological Awareness Assessment

Phonological awareness is the ability to identify and analyze various parts of speech as they occur in spoken language. A child with strong phonological awareness can *blend* spoken sound units (syllables, onsets and rimes, or phonemes) to form words, or *segment* words into their constituent parts. (See Figure 1–8.) The ability to blend typically develops before the ability to segment (Yopp 1992). One main reason that phonological awareness is important is that when children are aware that words can be blended and segmented *orally*, they can use this knowledge to write and read words. However, the relationship between phonological awareness and phonics knowledge is not linear, but *reciprocal*. Working with words *in print* facilitates phonological awareness (National Reading Panel 2000; Stanovich 1986). Because phonological awareness is one of those easy-to-measure competencies, RTI teachers should exercise caution if using this assessment as a monitoring tool. Narrow, easy-to-measure items can run the risk of leading to a too-narrow instructional focus.

The Phonological Awareness Assessment is typically used in preschool, kindergarten, and first grade, and sometimes with older students who express difficulty with word analysis. Many teachers reserve phonological awareness assessments only for students who express difficulty with phonics. That is, if letter-sound knowledge or word analysis is not progressing as expected, assessing phonological awareness may offer some insight. Part 2 contains a strand of instructional practices for students needing support developing phonological awareness.

Figure 1–8 *Phonological Awareness*

A student with strong phonological awareness can:	
Blend syllables	*/ship/ /ment/* into *shipment*
Blend onsets with rimes	*/sh/ /ip/* into *ship*
Blend phonemes	*/sh/ /i/ /p/* into *ship*
Segment words into syllables	*shipment* into */ship/ /ment/*
Segment onsets from rimes	*ship* into */sh/ /ip/*
Segment phonemes	*ship* into */sh/ /i/ /p/*

Phonological Awareness Assessment

Name: _____ Date: _____

Syllabification

I'm going to say some words, and you break them into syllables. (Give credit for reasonable responses such as /buh/ /ter/ /fly/ even if they are not technically correct.)

Let's practice: If I say *market*, you say . . . /mar/ /ket/. (Tap each syllable.)

Other practice words: *insect, butterfly, caterpillar.*

sunshine __/2	*pollen* __/2	*flower* __/2	*abdomen* __/3
deliver __/3	*manufacture* __/4	*catastrophe* __/4	

Blending

I'm going to say some sounds, and you tell me the word they make.

Let's practice: If I say /t/ /a/ /g/, you say . . . *tag.*

Other practice words: *me, fine.*

/o/ /n/ (*on*) __/2	/i/ /t/ (*it*) __/2	/b/ /e/ /d/ (*bed*) __/3	/g/ a/ m/ (*game*) __/3
/c/ /u/ /p/ (*cup*)___/3	/l/ /i/ /t/ (*light*) __/3	/f/ /l/ /o/ /t/ (*float*) __/4	

Segmenting

I'm going to say a word and you break the word apart.

Let's practice: If I say *bug*, you say /b/ /u/ /g/.

Other practice words: *dog, man.*

if (/i/ /f/) __/2	*at* (/a/ /t/) __/2	*ship* (/sh/ /i/ /p/) __/3	*rock* (/r/ /o/ /k/) __/3
five (/f/ /i/ /v/) __/3	*then* (/th/ /e/ /n/) __/3	*glad* (/g/ /l/ /a/ /d/) __/4	

Date 1 _____	Date 2 _____	Date 3 _____	Date 4 _____
Syllabification: ____/20	Syllabification: ____/20	Syllabification: ____/20	Syllabification: ____/20
Blending: ____/20	Blending: ____/20	Blending: ____/20	Blending: ____/20
Segmenting:____/20	Segmenting: ____/20	Segmenting: ____/20	Segmenting: ____/20
Total: ____/60	Total: ____/60	Total: ____/60	Total: ____/60

Word Analysis: Features Assessment

Word analysis encompasses the ability to identify and analyze sound units (syllables, onsets, rimes, phonemes) as well as meaning units (root words and affixes). The importance of assessing word analysis throughout the elementary years should not be underestimated. Many students, even through high school, struggle with decoding multisyllabic words. Word analysis skills range from simple to complex:

- Early readers and readers who struggle may use only the first letter, or only the first and last letter, to decode an unknown word.

- As children develop their understanding of the alphabetic system, we can expect them to begin to use more letters, sometimes attempting to work their way through a word sound by sound (*g-a-r-d-e-n*) and/or blending the sounds to emerge with different pronunciations (*gare-deen*).

- As children develop further, they begin to use concepts of word parts and patterns (*g-ar-den*).

- Over time, readers develop yet more sophisticated concepts, such as the idea that multisyllabic words such as *reinvigorated* or *campaigning* can be decoded by dividing them into readable or meaningful parts (root words, syllables, prefixes, suffixes) and then putting the parts back together again.

Knowing the word-solving strategies your students try most often—and the phonic associations they control—can help you to meaningfully support their development toward more sophisticated strategies. Word analysis is typically assessed by observing and documenting what children do with unfamiliar words as they read aloud. When examining word-level miscues, useful instructional information can be gleaned by determining whether the reader is in control of the features listed on page 126. Part 2 contains a strand of instructional practices for students needing support developing word analysis.

Word Analysis: Feature Assessment

Name: _____ Date: _____

Document miscues as you listen to the student read. Look for patterns of error at the word level. Place a check next to any observed areas that could use instructional attention.

____ consonants

Parts examined in miscued words (use tallies):

____ consonant blends

Beginning: _____

____ consonant digraphs

Middle: _____

____ vowels

End:_____

____ rimes

____ affixes

____ multisyllabic words

Spelling Inventory

Word analysis is also assessed through observing students' spelling knowledge. Because spellers and readers draw from common orthographic base, insights into what a student is doing with spelling can provide insights into what the student is doing with reading. The Spelling Inventory (pages 128–132) can be used to gain a quick picture of your students' control over word features.

Spelling Inventory

Name: _____ Date: _____

Read aloud each word to the student and use it in a sentence. The student should write each word on a separate paper. (See Spelling Inventory: Student Form.) To evaluate, write the child's spelling next to the correct spelling below and then circle the known parts on the Feature Analysis chart. Kindergarten students may be asked to spell 1–5 or 1–10. First-grade students may be asked to spell 1–10 or 1–15. Older students may be asked to spell 6–20.

	Word	Child's Spelling		Word	Child's Spelling
1	sat		11	thorny	
2	led		12	charted	
3	win		13	flashlights	
4	hop		14	fastest	
5	bug		15	drawing	
6	quake		16	beginner	
7	life		17	differently	
8	cove		18	scurries	
9	years		19	traction	
10	zoom		20	incredible	

Feature Analysis

Consonants Items 1–10	S T L D W N H P B G QU K L F C V Y R Z M	___/20
Short Vowels Items 1–5	A E I O U	___/5
Vowel Combinations Items 6–13	a-e i-e o-e ea oo or ar igh	___/8
Consonant Blends and Doubles Items 13–20	FL ST DR NN FF SC TR CR	___/8
Consonant Digraphs Items 11–13	TH CH SH	___/3
Endings Items 11–20	Y ED S EST ING ER LY IES ION IBLE	___/10
Rimes Items 1–15	AT ED IN OP UG AKE IFE OVE EAR OOM ORN ART ASH AST AW	___/15

Spelling Inventory

Name: _____   Date: _____

Read aloud each word to the student and use it in a sentence. The student should write each word on a separate paper. (See Spelling Inventory: Student Form.) To evaluate, write the child's spelling next to the correct spelling below and then circle the known parts on the Feature Analysis chart. Kindergarten students may be asked to spell 1–5 or 1–10. First-grade students may be asked to spell 1–10 or 1–15. Older students may be asked to spell 6–20.

	Word	Child's Spelling		Word	Child's Spelling
1	sat	sat	11	thorny	thornee
2	led	led	12	charted	chartid
3	win	wine	13	flashlights	flashlits
4	hop	hop	14	fastest	fastist
5	bug	bug	15	drawing	groing
6	quake	qak	16	beginner	beedenr
7	life	lif	17	differently	difrintlee
8	cove	cov	18	scurries	skreeis
9	years	uers	19	traction	chrakshin
10	zoom	zoom	20	incredible	inkredbl

Feature Analysis		
Consonants Items 1–10	(S) (T) (L) (D) (W) (N) (H) (P) (B) (G) QU (K) (L) (F) (C) (V) Y (R) (Z) (M)	18 /20
Short Vowels Items 1–5	(A) (E) I (O) (U)	4 /5
Vowel Combinations Items 6–13	a-e i-e o-e ea (oo) (or) (ar) igh	3 /8
Consonant Blends and Doubles Items 13–20	(FL) (ST) DR NN FF SC TR CR	2 /8
Consonant Digraphs Items 11–13	(TH) (CH) (SH)	3 /3
Endings Items 11–20	Y ED (S) EST (ING) ER LY IES ION IBLE	2 /10
Rimes Items 1–15	(AT) (ED) IN (OP) (UG) AKE IFE OVE EAR (OOM) (ORN) (ART) (ASH) (AST) AW	9 /15

Spelling Inventory: Example

SPELLING INVENTORY

Name: Emilia

Date: 3/31   Date: 5/15

1. SATe	1. Sat
2. LED	2. LeD
3. WINe	3. WINe
4. hop	4. HOP
5. BUG	5. BUG
6. QAKe	6. QAK
7. LIF	7. LIF
8. KOve	8. COV
9. yeRS	9. UeRS
10. Soom	10. Soom
11. thoRNee	11. fhoRNee
12. chARpID	12. c hARtID
13. FLAShLIs	13. FLAShLits
14. FAStISt	14. FAStist
15. gROING	15. GROING
16. BeegeNR	16. BReGeNR.
17. DIFRItLee	17. DIFRINtLeE
18. SkRees	18. SkRees
19. chRAKdnINmAN	19. chRAKShiN
20. INCREDBLL	20. INKReDBL

130

Spelling Inventory: Student Form

Name: _____

Date: _____   Date: _____

1. _____   1. _____

2. _____   2. _____

3. _____   3. _____

4. _____   4. _____

5. _____   5. _____

6. _____   6. _____

7. _____   7. _____

8. _____   8. _____

9. _____   9. _____

10. _____   10. _____

11. _____   11. _____

12. _____   12. _____

13. _____   13. _____

14. _____   14. _____

15. _____   15. _____

16. _____   16. _____

17. _____   17. _____

18. _____   18. _____

19. _____   19. _____

20. _____   20. _____

Spelling Inventory Scores

For each student, take note of patterns of error on the Spelling Inventory. Place a check in the boxes below to indicate next steps for instruction. Group students accordingly.

	Child's Name	Consonants	Short Vowels	Vowel Combinations	Consonant Blends and Doubles	Consonant Digraphs	Endings	Rimes
1								
2								
3								
4								
5								
6								
7								
8								
9								
10								
11								
12								
13								
14								
15								
16								
17								
18								
19								
20								
21								
22								
23								
24								
25								
26								
27								
28								
29								
30								

High-Frequency Word Inventory

High-frequency word recognition may be assessed throughout the elementary years, though many teachers formally assess it only when students are not successfully reading grade-level text. The *High-Frequency Word Inventory* (developed from Fry's High-Frequency Word List 1997) is a quick way to formally gather information about the words students know (and don't know), as well as the automaticity with which they read them. Another, less formal, way to assess high-frequency word knowledge is to document miscues as students read classroom text. As you analyze the miscues, note whether sight words are causing particular difficulty. The Reading Assessment may be used for this purpose.

Automaticity is taken into consideration when assessing word knowledge because text processing is most efficient when students recognize words instantly, without needing to use word analysis strategies to identify them. It is generally recognized that when words are automatically known, more attentional resources are available for the reader to focus on comprehending (LaBerge and Samuels 1974).

High-Frequency Words

About 50 percent of the words that children encounter in print are found on the list of the one hundred most frequently used words in the English language (page 134). This means that if students know the hundred words on the list, they know about half of the words they encounter as they read. About 65 percent of the words children encounter in print are found on the list of three hundred most frequently used words. Therefore, knowing some high-frequency words is extremely important for young readers; it provides an important "foothold" as they begin to work their way through text (Calkins 2001).

First Hundred Words

Name: _____   **Date:** _____

High-Frequency Word Inventory: First Hundred

First 25		Second 25	Third 25		Fourth 25
the		or	will		number
of		one	up		no
and		had	other		way
a		by	about		could
to		word	out		people
in		but	many		my
is		not	then		than
you		what	them		first
that		all	these		water
it		were	so		been
he		we	some		call
was		when	her		who
for		your	would		oil
on		can	make		now
are		said	like		find
as		there	him		long
with		use	into		down
his		an	time		day
they		each	has		did
I		which	look		get
at		she	two		come
be		do	more		made
this		how	write		may
have		their	go		part
from		if	see		over
Date: _____ ____/25 Date: _____ ____/25		Date: _____ ____/25 Date: _____ ____/25	Date: _____ ____/25 Date: _____ ____/25		Date: _____ ____/25 Date: _____ ____/25

Second Hundred Words

Name: _____ Date: _____

High-Frequency Word Inventory: Second Hundred

101–125	126–150	151–175	176–200
new	great	put	kind
sound	where	end	hand
take	help	does	picture
only	through	another	again
little	much	well	change
work	before	large	off
know	line	must	play
place	right	big	spell
year	too	even	air
live	mean	such	away
me	old	because	animal
back	any	turn	house
give	same	here	point
most	tell	why	page
very	boy	ask	letter
after	follow	went	mother
thing	came	men	answer
our	want	read	found
just	show	need	study
name	also	land	still
good	around	different	learn
sentence	form	home	should
man	three	us	America
think	small	move	world
say	set	try	high
Date: _____ ____/25 Date: _____ ____/25	Date: _____ ____/25 Date: _____ ____/25	Date: _____ ____/25 Date: _____ ____/25	Date: _____ ____/25 Date: _____ ____/25

Third Hundred Words

Name: _____   Date: _____

High-Frequency Word Inventory: Third Hundred

201–225	226–250	251–275	276–300
every	left	until	idea
near	don't	children	enough
add	few	side	eat
food	while	feet	face
between	along	car	watch
own	might	mile	far
below	close	night	Indian
country	something	walk	real
plant	seem	white	almost
last	next	sea	let
school	hard	began	above
father	open	grow	girl
keep	example	took	sometimes
tree	begin	river	mountain
never	life	four	cut
start	always	carry	young
city	those	state	talk
earth	both	once	soon
eye	paper	book	list
light	together	hear	song
thought	got	stop	leave
head	group	without	family
under	often	second	body
story	run	late	music
saw	important	miss	color
Date: _____ ____/25 Date: _____ ____/25	Date: _____ ____/25 Date: _____ ____/25	Date: _____ ____/25 Date: _____ ____/25	Date: _____ ____/25 Date: _____ ____/25

Miscue Documentation and Analysis

Documenting and analyzing miscues (deviations from text made while reading orally) is an ideal way to get to know students as readers (K. Goodman, 1996). For students who are in the early phases of developing text processing knowledge, and those who struggle, continued miscue documentation is recommended.

Phonics and *word knowledge* are an important part of what miscue analysis can reveal but these are not the only systems of information that young readers bring to their text processing. Readers also use *syntactic* and *semantic* cues. Syntactic cues allow the reader to predict words based on what might *sound right* and semantic cues allow the reader to predict based on what might *make sense*. For example, in reading *Julio* _____ *the dog's ear*, the reader can use *syntactic* cues to predict a verb, and *semantic* cues to predict something a person might do to a dog's ear.

Predicting helps young readers identify words by narrowing down what the print might say. If the text says, *Julio* <u>*stroked*</u> *the dog's ear* but the child reads, *Julio* <u>*scratched*</u> *the dog's ear*, we can tell that the reader is predicting or attending to meaning. However, if the child were to read *Julio* <u>*straw*</u> *the dog's ear* (with no self-correction), we could assume that syntactic and semantic cues were not being used, and this would be deemed a low-quality miscue.

In general, the quality of a miscue is judged by the degree to which it sustains the meaning and structure of the text. In most cases, as readers learn, they begin to make higher-quality miscues, and the number of miscues diminishes. From the start, we expect students to attempt to correct miscues that don't make sense or sound right. If their patterns of error show that they do not correct low-quality miscues, cue system instruction is warranted.

English language learners require special consideration when it comes to considering miscues. Just like native speakers, English language learners can be expected to think ahead and make predictions. However, in so doing, they may change the syntax to their own patterns and end up uttering syntactically unacceptable English sentences—which doesn't necessarily affect meaning. Given that the purpose of reading is not to identify words, but to construct meaning, teachers must consider differences between comprehension issues and linguistic issues when analyzing miscues. It is also important to note that English language learners may also be more likely to focus on analyzing words than to predict using semantics and syntax, given that their knowledge of English is still developing (Ferguson et al. 2003; Goodman, Watson, and Burke 2005; Hadaway, Vardell, and Young 2004).

tracking chart for Quantitative Changes in Fluency over Time (page 143). As a cautionary note, quantitative fluency measures should be accompanied by other, more qualitative measures that do not rely only on speed and accuracy.

When assessing fluency, it is important to keep in mind that low fluency is often secondary to other reading issues. For example, students with low fluency often demonstrate difficulty with word analysis, automatic recognition of sight words, and/or effective use of cue systems. These "primary" issues cause a "secondary" problem with fluency. Part 2 contains strands of instructional practices for students needing support developing varying aspects of fluency.

The Qualitative Dimensions of Fluency Rubric

Record the text, text level, and date. Observe the student reading aloud and use the rubric to designate whether the student demonstrates high, medium, or low fluency for the piece. Also ask one or two questions to develop insight into the student's comprehension.

Possible prompts for assessing comprehension: What did the author teach? What happened?

Student: _____   Date: _____

Text: _____   Text Level: _____

Comprehension			
Understandings Demonstrated	Low	Medium	High
	Few key concepts or ideas mentioned	Some key concepts or ideas mentioned	Key concepts or ideas mentioned

Fluency			
Elements of Fluency Demonstrated	Low	Medium	High
• Phrasing	Little or no meaningful phrasing	Some reading in meaningful phrases	Reads in meaningful phrases, attending to punctuation
• Smoothness • Pace	Little or no smooth reading and conversational pacing	Some smooth reading and conversational pacing	Reads smoothly, at a conversational pace
• Expression	Little or no natural or expressive reading	Some expressive reading	Reads expressively, varying expression as appropriate

Fluency rubric based on Rasinski (2004).

The Quantitative Dimension of Fluency Scale: Appropriate Ranges for Words Correct Per Minute

Observe the student reading aloud a grade-level text. Record the text, text level, and date. Use the rubric to designate the student's words correct per minute (WCPM) and to determine whether the student falls within the expected range for the grade level.

Grade	Fall WCPM	Winter WCPM	Spring WCPM
1			40 minimum
2	41–61	62–82	79–99
3	61–81	82–102	97–117
4	84–104	92–122	113–133
5	100–120	117–137	129–149

Based on research conducted by Hasbrouck and Tindal (2006).

Notes:

Quantitative Changes in Fluency over Time

To observe quantitative changes in fluency, choose four carefully leveled texts (one for each quarter) and use them to assess the number of words read correctly per minute. Use the same level over time, rather than moving to harder text as students develop. The level can be chosen based on the grade you teach or based on initial assessments.

List Children's Names	Text Level Used	First Quarter	Second Quarter	Third Quarter	Fourth Quarter

© 2010 by Gretchen Owocki, from *The RTI Daily Planning Book, K–6.* Portsmouth, NH: Heinemann.

143

Comprehension Strategy and Think-Aloud Observations

Just as it can be useful to observe specific knowledge and strategies related to text processing, it can be useful to interact with students and observe their knowledge and strategies related to text comprehending. It is generally agreed upon that readers construct meaning through a combination of comprehension strategies—monitoring, questioning, using background knowledge and connections, drawing inferences, visualizing, evaluating, and summarizing key ideas—and through talking with others in relation to these strategies. The strategies are used simultaneously and discriminately: instead of using them just one at a time, readers use all of them together, and depending on the event, some are emphasized more than others. Even beginners use reading comprehension strategies; kids are just too curious about the world to wait for fluency to occur before developing strategies for comprehending. When working with students who generally demonstrate low comprehension, it is important to understand that successful comprehenders have more strategies available than unsuccessful comprehenders (Walczyk 2000) and use them more purposefully.

In order to gain insight into students' comprehension, we need not assess every comprehension strategy or behavior. Usually, interacting with the student and looking for evidence that the student is using one or two strategies allows us to determine that the others are in place. For example, if a student can provide a detailed *summary* or *synthesis*, this is an indication that the student has *monitored*, *drawn the necessary inferences*, *made use of background knowledge*, and so on. Of all of the strategies, summarizing (or retelling) is used most often for assessing comprehension and is considered the most universally useful for determining a student's comprehension.

The Reading Assessment provides insights into comprehension from varying angles. It prompts students to provide a summary, a connection to background knowledge, and an inference. While these prompts offer insights into what students are doing with comprehension, we can't wait for comprehension questions at the ends of passages to do our assessing. It is through continued observation and spontaneous but thoughtful interaction that we obtain the information we need to encourage and support thoughtful literacy.

Key comprehension strategies to observe and discuss with students on an ongoing basis appear on page 146. A set of prompts is suggested along with each strategy so that you can plan to listen as students think aloud about the meaning they are constructing, and how they are constructing it. A note-taking form to guide informal observation is featured on page 147. This form may be used to take anecdotal notes and to ensure that you are spacing out your observations among all of the readers in your classroom— or among all of the readers in your intervention groups. Classroom teachers and intervention specialists may use the form to compare observations and plan next steps in instruction.

Strategy	Examples of Think-Aloud Prompts
Questioning. Proficient readers are always generating *questions* as they read. They ask, What's going to happen? What's coming next? What are the important ideas? How do these ideas fit together? When proficient readers want to know something in particular, they have strategies for seeking the answer.	What are you wondering right now? How do you think you will find out about that? Where will you find the answer?
Monitoring. Effective readers *monitor* their comprehension. While reading, they actively focus on tracking meaning: they think through where the text has been so far and where it might go next. When meaning starts to waver, they recognize it and use repair strategies to get back on track. Repair strategies typically involve rereading, self-correcting, reading on, slowing down, considering punctuation, looking at the illustrations, checking to see if the text structure or format gives any clues, and pinpointing any confusing words or phrases.	What did you do to get ready for reading this text? Summarize or retell what you've read. When you were stuck, how did you solve your problem? What do you predict will come next?
Connecting. *Connections* happen when readers link elements of their personal knowledge, experiences, and understandings with the text they are reading, in ways that enhance understanding.	What do you know about this topic? Have you ever seen or experienced something like this?
Drawing Inferences. Authors don't tell us everything we need to know. Some things must be inferred. *Inferring* involves supplying the information that is not explicitly stated in the text. For example, even though the author doesn't state it directly we might *infer* that a character is brave, a female, or a school teacher because of the actions she takes.	What might the author mean by this? What does the author assume we know? Why might the author have written this? What is the author referring to?
Visualizing. When readers *visualize*, they create mental images that draw from what they have experienced in the world. Visualizing involves evoking images not only of the sights, but also of the sounds, smells, tastes, and emotions suggested by the text. Creating this "living picture" helps students to understand text and experience it more deeply.	Describe what is happening here. What do you see in your mind?
Evaluating. *Evaluating* is a strategy that encompasses a wide range of thinking, including critiquing, establishing opinions, and considering how information from text might be used and applied. When students demonstrate thoughtful evaluations that draw sufficiently from information within the text, they are providing evidence for meaningful comprehending.	What do you think about this piece—and why? Do you agree with this author's views? Do the characters seem real? How can you use the information from this text?
Determining and Summarizing Key Ideas. *Determining key ideas* is critical to effective reading. Books contain many interesting things to pay attention to but—quite often—homing in on certain ideas is beneficial. For example, with stories, when children learn to focus on features such as characters, setting, problem, events, and resolution, they have learned to capture the gist of the piece. With nonfiction, when children learn to focus on key text structures such as comparison, time order, or problem resolution, they have a mental framework for discussing, rethinking, and remembering the ideas. Summarizing and synthesizing are important because they involve students in bringing their ideas to a conscious level where they can talk about and rethink them and where their teachers can actively monitor whether important parts have been understood.	What has happened so far? What has the author taught? What is this about? What new ideas or understandings have you developed?

Comprehension Strategy and Think-Aloud Observations	
Students Observed	Evidence for Use of Comprehension Strategies

Comprehension After Listening Assessment

Listening to text read aloud is an important part of learning in many classrooms. If you have concerns about any of your students' listening comprehension, you may wish to explore it with a specialized assessment. The *Comprehension After Listening Assessment* can be implemented with one student (questions are answered orally) or with a small group or whole class (questions are answered in writing).

1. Select a text used for instruction in your classroom (fiction or nonfiction). Or use one of the texts on the recommended booklist for assessment. If you select one of your own texts, be sure that fiction choices have clear problem-resolution sequences. If you select nonfiction, be sure to use a short section that is manageable for a retelling.

2. Have available the appropriate Listening Comprehension Form and Rubric (fiction or nonfiction) (page 149 or 151).

3. Read the text aloud and engage the student in discussion or writing related to the comprehension questions.

4. Fill out the rubric.

Listening Comprehension: Fiction

Name: _____ Date: _____ Text: _____

What do you know about (name the topic)?

STUDENT LISTENS TO TEXT OR PORTION OF TEXT

What is this story/selection about?

What was a problem? What did the character(s) do about that?

Think of something you have experienced like this. Tell about it.

Look at this illustration (or listen to these sentences) and tell what you think the character was feeling at that point.

Element	Level or Content May Be Too Challenging	Good for Instruction	Independent
• Characters • Problem or goal	A critical problem or goal of a key character is not adequately identified.	Partially describes a critical problem or goal of a key character.	Describes most/all relevant aspects of a critical problem or goal of a key character.
• Events • Solution	Does not adequately identify key events.	Accurately retells some key events.	Accurately retells key events, including solution.
• Prior knowledge • Connections	Demonstrates little prior knowledge; connections show little depth.	Demonstrates some prior knowledge; connects on lower levels to ideas or themes in text.	Demonstrates prior knowledge; expresses a connection to ideas or themes in text.
• Inferences	No demonstrated inferences.	Demonstrates some inferring.	Demonstrates relevant, insightful inferences that have support in the text.

Name: **Ahmad**   Date:_____   Text: **Mercy Watson**

Listening Comprehension: Fiction

What do you know about (name the topic?)

Pigs eat a lot

STUDENT LISTENS TO TEXT OR PORTION OF TEXT

What is this story/selection about?

A Pig wanted to drive.

What was a problem? What did the character(s) do about that?

She wanted to drive. She pushed in and drove.

Think of something you have experienced like this. Tell me about it.

My dog is pushy.

Look at this illustration (or listen to these sentences) and tell what you think the character was feeling at that point.

Happy to drive.

Element	Level or content may be too challenging	Good for instruction	Independent
• Characters • Problem or goal	A critical problem or goal of a key character is not identified.	Partially describes a critical problem or goal of a key character.	Describes most/all relevant aspects of a critical problem or goal of a key character.
• Events • Solution	Does not adequately identify key events.	Accurately retells some key events.	Accurately retells key events, including solution.
• Prior knowledge • Connections	Demonstrates little prior knowledge; connections show little depth.	Demonstrates some prior knowledge; connects on lower levels to ideas or themes in text.	Demonstrates prior knowledge; expresses a connection to ideas or themes in text.
• Inferences	No demonstrated inferences.	Demonstrates some inferring.	Demonstrates relevant, insightful inferences.

Listening Comprehension: Nonfiction

Name: _____ Date: _____ Text: _____

What do you know about (name the topic)?

STUDENT LISTENS TO TEXT OR PORTION OF TEXT

What did the author teach about in this book/selection?

Tell more about that.

Think of something you have experienced/seen like this. Tell about it.

Why do you think the author wrote this book?

Element	Level or Content May Be Too Challenging	Good for Instruction	Independent
• Synthesis	Does not identify main idea.	Synthesis partially captures overall idea of text.	Synthesizes the overall idea of the text.
• Determining key ideas	Does not identify key aspects of what the author taught.	Accurately identifies some key aspects of what the author taught.	Accurately identifies most/all key aspects of what the author taught.
• Prior knowledge • Connections	Demonstrates little prior knowledge; connections show little depth.	Demonstrates some prior knowledge; connects on lower levels to ideas or themes in text.	Demonstrates prior knowledge; expresses a connection to ideas in text.
• Inferences	No demonstrated inferences.	Demonstrates some inferring.	Demonstrates relevant, insightful inferences that have support in the text.

Fiction Versus Nonfiction Assessment

When compared with fiction, nonfiction can present some unique challenges for readers. Nonfiction text structure is not always as evident as it is with fiction, the content is often not as personal or familiar (Caldwell 2002), and the text structures vary more widely. All of this can make comprehension of nonfiction a challenge. To determine whether a student has particular difficulty negotiating nonfiction, you can use the Reading Assessment to see if the reader tests at approximately the same level for both fiction and nonfiction. If one area is stronger than the other, you know where to place your instructional emphasis.

Question Types Assessment

Assessing responses to different question types will help you determine whether your students can answer both literal and higher-level questions. Lower-order questions typically require that students state remembered facts and events. Higher-order questions involve the use of higher-order comprehension processes such as drawing inferences, determining important ideas, synthesizing ideas, and evaluating, defending, and justifying with text (as listed on the Comprehension Strategy and Think-Aloud Observations chart (page 146).

General Story Map with Rubric

Story maps can be used as a tool for assessing elements of story comprehension. The General Story Map (page 155) guides students to identify four basic elements: characters, setting, problem, and resolution. Students can be asked to draw and/or write on the map. It is a good idea to model the use of a story map before using it as an assessment tool. This will help students to understand your expectations.

To implement this assessment, you may use texts recommended for the Reading Assessment or texts of your own choosing. When choosing your own texts, be sure that the four elements are included. (Some fiction is not organized using these four features.) When analyzing student work, keep in mind that writing may get in the way of what you can glean regarding a student's comprehension. Students who comprehend a text may not necessarily be able to organize their ideas about it in writing.

Another option is to have students think-aloud as they "build" the story using sticky notes. Students can place the notes in an arc to represent the rising and falling action.

General Story Map

Name: _____ Date: _____

Title

Important Characters	Setting

Problem or Goal	Solution

Element	May Be Too Challenging	Good for Instruction	Independent
Characters	Shows little understanding of key characters.	Includes some key characters.	Includes key characters.
Setting	Relevant aspects of setting not evident.	Includes some or somewhat relevant aspects of setting.	Includes relevant aspects of setting.
Problem or goal	A problem or goal of a key character not identified.	Partially shows a problem/goal of a key character.	Shows relevant aspects of a problem/goal of a key character.
Solution	Solution not clearly featured.	Solution somewhat featured.	Solution clearly featured.

General Story Map: Example

Name: Javon   **Date:** 10-2   **Text:** The Mystery of the Cheese

General Story Map

Title

Important Characters	Setting
maN mom Cid Doe	oshiv

Problem or Goal	Solution
He Tht The mooN woss a Biə pese ov cheesl..	The mooN wuss vt a pes av chees

Element	May be too challenging	Good for instruction	Independent
Characters	Shows little understanding of key characters.	Includes some key characters.	Includes key characters.
Setting	Relevant aspects of setting not evident.	Includes some or somewhat relevant aspects of setting.	Includes relevant aspects of setting.
Problem or goal	A problem or goal of a key character not identified.	Partially shows a problem/goal of a key character.	Shows relevant aspects of a problem/goal of a key character.
Solution	Solution not clearly featured.	Solution somewhat featured.	Solution clearly featured.

Key Idea Map with Rubric

Key idea maps can be used as a tool for assessing student understandings related to nonfiction text. The Key Idea Map (page 158) guides students to synthesize what the piece/section was about and then provide some detail. Students can be asked to draw and/or write on the map. It is a good idea to model the use of a key idea map before using it as an assessment tool. This will help students understand what is expected.

To implement this assessment, you may use texts recommended for the Reading Assessment or texts of your own choosing. When choosing text, be sure that the segment you ask students to read lends itself to a synthesis and listing of key concepts taught. When analyzing student work, keep in mind that writing may get in the way of what you can glean regarding a student's comprehension. Students who comprehend a text may not necessarily be able to organize their ideas about it in writing.

Key Idea Map

Name: _____ Date: _____

Title: _____ Pages: _____

What did the author teach?

Explain something important about a concept that the author taught.

Element	Level or Content May Be Too Challenging	Good for Instruction	Independent
Synthesis	Does not identify main idea.	Synthesis partially captures overall idea of text.	Synthesizes the overall idea of the text.
Determining key ideas	Does not identify a key aspect of what the author taught.	Chooses and explains part of an important concept.	Chooses and explains an important concept.

Name: Aurora   Date: 9/7

Key Idea Map

Title: Ice Mummy   Pages: 48

What did the author teach?
every day. New discoverys can be found

Explain something important the author taught about that.
If you look very ~~carfuly~~ you may
find a piece of history.

Element	Level or content may be too challenging	Good for instruction	Independent
Synthesis	Does not identify main idea.	Synthesis partially captures overall idea of text.	Synthesizes the overall idea of the text.
Determining Key Ideas	Does not identify a key aspect of what the author taught.	Chooses and explains part of an important concept.	Chooses and explains an important concept.

Name: Diego   Date: 3-02   _____

Key Idea Map

Title: _____ Pages:_____

What did the author teach?

DBOWT TODPLS

Explain something important the author taught about that.

The todpls come out of jelly.

Element	Level or content may be too challenging	Good for instruction	Independent
Synthesis	Does not identify main idea.	Synthesis partially captures overall idea of text.	Synthesizes the overall idea of the text.
Determining Key Ideas	Does not identify a key aspect of what the author taught.	Chooses and explains part of an important concept.	Chooses and explains an important concept.

Vocabulary and Conceptual Knowledge Assessment

Along with observing for student use of comprehension strategies, it is often enlightening to consider students' background knowledge for the texts they are reading. "Full comprehension of written text requires knowledge of the language, knowledge of the world, and knowledge of subject-specific vocabulary" (Dudley-Marling and Paugh 2004, 59). Though a student may be a strong comprehender in general, reading material that is focused on unfamiliar concepts and uses unknown vocabulary can make comprehension skills appear to be lacking. For students who can decode well but consistently have difficulty comprehending nonfiction, you may want to distinguish whether it is *comprehension skills* or *vocabulary and conceptual knowledge* (or both) that need support because these generally require different instructional emphases. Careful assessments of vocabulary knowledge related to the piece can generally help to make this distinction. Ask your students:

* What do you know about this topic?

* What experience do you have with it?

* What are some words you associate with this topic?

* How familiar are you with these words?

Vocabulary Knowledge Assessment

Working with an individual or a small group, choose six to eight subject-specific vocabulary words from the text to be read. List the words for the student(s) to view. At this point, you may wish to ask students how well they know each word. They may rate them using the following scale:

1 – I know this word and can use it in a sentence.

2 – I have heard this word and have some idea what it means.

3 – I don't know the meaning of this word.

Engage the student(s) in a discussion focused on what they know about each word. Take note of which words the students know, and which students may need extra support to comprehend the reading.

2

Instructional Practices and Tools

Getting Started:
A Framework for Instruction

The *Instructional Practices* section features a comprehensive set of strategies that will facilitate your teaching and differentiation of instruction in all areas of reading. The strategies are presented in *strands* that match the text processing and text comprehending assessment categories featured in Part 1. Tracing the strands from Part 1 to Part 2 will enable you to match your instruction with the specific student needs you have identified through the assessments. See the If-Then Chart for Instruction in Text Processing and Text Comprehending for specific ways to match identified needs with instructional practices. Some of the practices are designed to be implemented in small groups, some are designed for the whole class, and others can be enacted with little teacher presence. All of the reproducible forms can be found online (under the Companion Resources tab on the book's product page on the Heinemann website).

A workshop or center-based approach can easily encompass the teaching strategies and processes you will find in Part 2. A typical workshop or center-based approach involves a daily read-aloud or demonstration with a minilesson, and then extended time for independent or group activities while the teacher provides small-group instruction. While the teacher is working with groups, different students' activities may involve team projects, center activities, literature discussion groups, writing experiences, and independent or paired reading. All of the instructional strategies are designed to support the components of such a daily structure.

Guided reading is recommended as a daily form of small-group instruction. Lesson plans for groups within RTI classrooms are included along with many other experiences that can be nested into the work of small groups. The teaching team can use the RTI lesson planning forms (pages 219–220 and 233–234) to plan needs-based small-group lessons and to document and share observations. To make the small-group/intervention sessions as robust as possible, the classroom teacher and intervention teacher should make it a regular practice to (1) plan together and (2) teach toward the same concepts using similar routines and instructional language. The RTI lesson planning forms can be used to facilitate these processes.

If-Then Chart for Instruction in Text Processing and Text Comprehending

If Students Need Support in These Strands . . .		Then Try These Strategies	Page	Whole Class	Small Group/ Individual	Centers or Teams
Text Processing	Print Concept Knowledge	Modeled Reading with a Focus on Print Concepts	169	X	X	
		Shared Reading with a Focus on Print Concepts	170	X	X	
		Interactive Writing	171	X	X	
		Environmental Print Study	172	X		X
		Environmental Print Big Books	173	X		X
		Literacy Walks	174	X		
		Environmental Print Wordplay	174		X	X
		Reading the Walls	175	X		X
		Paired Book Sharing	175	X		X
	Letter Knowledge	Modeled Writing with an Emphasis on Letters	176	X	X	
		Shared Writing with an Emphasis on Letters	176	X	X	
		Scaffolded Writing	177		X	
		Name Cards	177	X	X	
		Word Cards	178	X	X	
		Structured Letter Play	179			X
		Manipulating Letters	180	X	X	X
		Alphabet Strips	180	X		
		Alphabet Book Study	183	X		X
		Alphabet Mat Activities	183		X	X
	Phonological Awareness	Oral Language Study	188	X	X	
		Modeled Writing with an Emphasis on Listening for Sounds	188	X	X	
		Scaffolded Spelling	189	X	X	
		Object Sorts	190		X	X
		Onset-Rime Lessons	190	X	X	
		Rhyme Lessons	194	X	X	
		Sound Boxes	194		X	
		Say It and Move It	202		X	

If-Then Chart for Instruction in Text Processing and Text Comprehending

If Students Need Support in These Strands . . .		Then Try These Strategies	Page	Whole Class	Small Group/ Individual	Centers or Teams
Text Processing	Phonics Knowledge and Word Analysis	Word Study	204	X	X	
		Word Sorts	205		X	X
		Student-Made Alphabet Books	206	X		
		Word Hunts	206			X
		Word Challenges	207			X
		Word Building	207		X	
		Scaffolded Writing	208		X	
	Decoding Multisyllabic Words	Syllable and Part Blending	209	X	X	
		Parts Analysis	211		X	
		Spelling in Parts	211	X	X	
		Tricky Passages	212		X	
		Word Recording	212		X	X
	High-Frequency Words	Word Study and Word Wall	213	X	X	
		Visual-Auditory-Kinesthetic-Tactile Approach	214		X	
		Manipulating Words	214		X	
		Transparency Tape Lists	215		X	
		Word Concentration	215			X
		Retrospective Miscue Analysis: High-Frequency Words	215		X	
	Using and Integrating Cue Systems	Guided Reading	217		X	
		Cue System Prompts	221	X	X	
		Miscue Investigation	221		X	
		Retrospective Miscue Analysis	223		X	
		Cooperative Controlled Cloze	224	X	X	
	Fluency	Independent Reading	225			X
		Repeated Reading	225			X
		Echo Reading	225		X	

166

If-Then Chart for Instruction in Text Processing and Text Comprehending						
If Students Need Support in These Strands . . .		**Then Try These Strategies**	**Page**	**Whole Class**	**Small Group/ Individual**	**Centers or Teams**
Text Processing	Fluency	Paired Reading	226			X
		Team Reading	226			X
		Computer and Audio-Recorded Reading	226			X
		Performance Reading	226		X	
		Readers Theatre	227		X	X
		Documentary Clip Reading	227		X	X
		Fluency Development Lesson	228		X	
		Language Transcription	228		X	
Text Comprehending	Prereading	Three-Finger-Rule	230	X		
		Previewing	230	X	X	
	Engaging with Text	Guided Reading	232		X	
		Mindful Predicting	235	X	X	
		Mindful Questioning	237	X	X	
		Questioning the Author	238		X	
		Reciprocal Questioning	239		X	
		Mindful Monitoring	240	X	X	
		Reciprocal Teaching	242	X	X	
		Literature Circles	243			X
	Identifying Main/Key Ideas	Retelling Guides	245	X		X
		Story Maps	248	X		X
		Informational Text Maps	254	X		X
		Retelling Centers	266			X
	Thinking Beyond the Text	Mindful Inferring	267	X		
		Question Solving	269	X	X	
		Collaborative Reasoning	270		X	

If Students Need Support in These Strands . . .		Then Try These Strategies	Page	Whole Class	Small Group/ Individual	Centers or Teams
If-Then Chart for Instruction in Text Processing and Text Comprehending						
Text Comprehending	Content and Vocabulary Knowledge	Gathering Information	271	X		X
		What Do You Know Web	274	X	X	
		Question and Answer Generation	276	X	X	
		Preview, Overview, Review	276	X	X	
		Charting Questions and Answers	277	X		X
		Key Word Study	280	X	X	
		Vocabulary Studies	280	X	X	X
		Resources for New Words	288	X	X	
		Thematic Read-Alouds	288	X	X	
		Morphological Analysis	289		X	
		Language Structure Challenges	290		X	X
		Studying English Language Syntax	291		X	

For Students Needing Support Developing Print Concept Knowledge

Modeled Reading with a Focus on Print Concepts

Modeled reading is a teacher-led instructional technique that involves making explicit a planned set of key concepts. The focus of this lesson is on *early print concepts*. It should be implemented with students whose assessments reveal a need for support in this area. Depending on student needs, it can be implemented with the whole class or small groups.

1. Select a big book. Or, if working with a small group, any size book will suffice.

2. Introduce the book by previewing the title, author, and illustrations with the students. Turn through the first few pages (front matter) and ask students where you should begin reading. Work with students to find the appropriate page, and to find the first word of the story. When you find the first page, talk about the different functions that the print and illustrations serve. During the preview, use terms such as *title*, *author*, *cover*, *page*, *word*, *letter*, *illustrations*, and *beginning*. When working with English language learners, be sure to assess understanding regularly.

3. Read the text aloud to the students. When working with English language learners, be sure to use gestures, references to illustrations, and extended explanation as appropriate.

4. After reading, ask students, "What do you think?" or "What did the author teach?"

5. After discussing the content, turn back through the pages to discuss interesting or important words and punctuation. Reread a few key phrases or pages with the students, pointing to the words to show print directionality. Invite students to use highlighting tape or Wikki Stix to mark the words or punctuation.

6. Follow up with small groups or intervention groups as needed. Follow-ups should involve continuing the lesson with different books until the students demonstrate competency with the concepts and related terminology.

Shared Reading with a Focus on Print Concepts

Shared reading is a teacher-led instructional technique that involves the teacher and students reading together and discussing various concepts related to print. The focus of this shared reading lesson is on *early print concepts*. It should be implemented with students whose assessments reveal a need for support in this area. The procedures may be implemented with the whole class or small groups (depending on student needs).

1. Select a big book that is written at an appropriate level for student reading. Or if working with a small group, provide each child with a copy of the text.

2. Preview the title, author, and illustrations with students.

3. Read the text *to* the students as they follow along, and discuss the content with them. When working with English language learners, be sure to use gestures, references to illustrations, and extended explanation as appropriate.

4. Read the text *with* the students, emphasizing selected print concepts. Your choices will depend on what you have observed through the Print Concepts Assessment:

   - **Concept of directionality.** As you read, use a pointer to show left-to-right, top-to-bottom progression. Tell children what you are doing with the pointer and why. After you have modeled, ask volunteers to use the pointer to demonstrate directionality as you read together.

   - **Concept of letter and sound.** As you read, pause to discuss interesting words. Ask children to locate each word that is discussed and to tell how they found the word on the page. Use the opportunity to discuss letters and sounds.

   - **Concept of word.** As you read, use a pointer to show how sequences of spoken words match sequences of written words. Pause during the reading to name words and ask volunteers to use the pointer to show their location on the page. Help volunteers use Wikki Stix or highlighting tape to mark the words and to then use the pointer as you and the children read the whole sentence in which the word appears.

- **Concept of punctuation.** As you read, pause to point out how the author uses punctuation. Read chosen sentences aloud, using the intonation suggested by the punctuation.

- **Book handling terms.** As you read, pause at appropriate points to use common book-related terms, such as *author, illustrator, character, setting, problem, solution, beginning, ending, front, back, page, letter, word,* and *illustration.*

5. Allow students to read the books during center or workshop time.

6. Follow up with small groups or intervention groups as needed. Follow-ups should involve continuing the lesson with different books and different concepts until the students demonstrate sufficient competency.

Interactive Writing

Interactive writing is a teacher-guided experience that involves the teacher acting as scribe while modeling various writing concepts and seeking student input on what is written. Interactive writing may be implemented with small groups or the whole class.

1. Select a purpose for writing that will be meaningful to the participating students. For example, you may write a note, a list, or a sentence about something the class has observed or experienced.

2. Use chart paper or a whiteboard to model the writing as the group observes and contributes ideas. As it is appropriate, allow children to do some of the writing for you. Stress the following:

- the concepts that print carries meaning and that print and illustrations convey meanings in different ways

- the concept of print directionality (in English, left to right and top to bottom)

- the concept that there is a one-to-one correspondence between oral and written language

- the concept of a letter

- the concept that a letter makes a sound

- the concept of a word

- where to begin writing on the page

- the concept of punctuation

- the concept of organization (a list is organized differently than a note or sentence)

- the concept that written language serves a variety of functions

3. Follow up the interactive writing lesson by providing opportunities for students to do their own writing.

Environmental Print Study

An important part of children's developing print concepts is their coming to understand that they can begin to predict what words say by looking at their letters and shapes. *Environmental print studies* are teacher-guided experiences designed to build this foundational understanding. The studies begin with the whole class and then move to teams and centers.

1. Collect a set of environmental print logos that you think will be familiar to your students (restaurant signs, store signs, cookie packaging, candy wrappers, cereal boxes, game logos, toy logos, street signs). Make a book that features three or four logos per page. Prepare a photocopy of the book for each child, leaving a few blank pages.

2. Read the original copy of the book with your students. (They should be able to read most pages to you.) As you are reading the words together, point to the words from left to right. Talk about the letters in the words, and talk about the initial sounds in the words. Point out to students that they can read many words in the environment, and they should start looking for these and reading them whenever they can.

3. Show the students the books you have photocopied for them, including the blank pages. Ask them to collect more print that they can read from their own homes and add it to the blank pages. They can staple on extra pages if needed. (Send a note home to facilitate this process.) Have a deadline for sending the books back to school.

4. Place the students with a partner to read the print in the books and the print they have added.

5. As a follow-up or a center experience, have students make the words with magnetic letters or letter tiles. This will help them begin to rely less on context and more on the letters themselves.

Environmental Print Big Books

Environmental print big books can be used to support children's early development of many print concepts and may be a first step into meaningful school-based reading for many students. The books are created with teacher guidance and are then moved to the classroom library or book center. Depending on student need, they may occasionally be used as instructional reading material in small groups. These books quickly become class favorites and can be used again and again to teach print concepts.

1. Have each child bring in one piece of themed environmental print to contribute to a class book. For example, the theme might be *foods we eat, breakfast food, dinner food*, or *stores in our city*.

2. Make a cover page and then tape one logo to each page of the book. Or elevate the level of challenge by including the logo as part of a sentence. Following are some examples.

   * Our Favorite Foods

     _____ likes to eat (logo here).
     (logo here) is one of our favorite foods.

   * What We Eat for Breakfast

     _____ eats (logo here) for breakfast.
     (logo here) are/is a great way to start the day.

   * What We Eat for Dinner

     _____'s family eats (logo here).
     Have you ever tried (logo here)?

   * Stores in Our Town

     This is a store in our town: (logo here).
     _____'s family shops at (logo here).

3. Read the book as a class or group, emphasizing concepts of directionality, letters and sounds, words, punctuation, and book-handling terms such as *page, word*, and *letter*.

4. After reading with the students, make the book available in the classroom library or book center.

5. As a follow-up experience, you can use the books for guided reading. Variations of the books can be created within small groups. English language learners will benefit from the repetition and the rich visual context the books provide.

Literacy Walks (Bennett-Armistead, Duke, and Moses 2005)

Literacy walks are a strategy for encouraging children to consider the reasons for print in the environment and to support them as they begin to read this print. To implement a literacy walk, take a short stroll through the neighborhood or school, looking for print and talking about what you find. Ask questions such as "What do you think that sign is for?" "What do you think that says?" "Do you see a letter you know?" "What is the first letter in the word?" "What sound do you think it makes?"

Environmental Print Wordplay

Environmental print wordplay is a student-centered experience that may be implemented in small groups or centers. The activity is designed to support children's attention to the letters and sounds in words.

1. Collect and laminate approximately twenty-four different signs and logos (restaurant signs, store signs, cookie packaging, candy wrappers, cereal boxes, game logos, toy logos, street signs). Try to collect two of each logo/sign.

2. During center time, individuals or teams may do the following:

   - Read each word.

   - Match the pairs.

   - Match a hand-printed version of the word with the colorful logo version.

   - Make the words with magnetic letters or letter tiles.

   - Copy five to eight of the words on note cards and then read them without the colorful context.

   - Choose a word and draw a picture to show where the word appears in the environment. Spell out the word on the illustration.

Reading the Walls

Reading the walls may be implemented as a whole-class experience or during center time. The activity is designed to help students locate and share knowledge about the words in the room that they can read.

1. Arrange for students to work with a partner and a pointer.

2. Teams walk around the room pointing to and reading words. Teams may be asked to record a set number of words they can read or would like to be able to read.

3. As an option, the students' documentation may be shared at group time.

Paired Book Sharing

Paired book sharing is a way to encourage students to explore print concepts in an informal setting, and it is a natural medium for children to enjoy the motivation that choosing their own texts creates. It may be implemented during center time, or as a whole-class project.

1. Have available a bin of books. Let students know that they will be reading in pairs. Select one student with whom to model. The modeling will be especially important for English language learners, who may not grasp all of your verbal instructions but will get a feel for the expectations through the modeling. Ask the student to choose a book from the bin. Sit together and look for the title, and then turn through the pages of the book together, talking about the illustrations and looking for interesting words or words the students may recognize.

2. Assign partners and then allow students to choose their own books and browse them together. Encourage the teams to look for the titles, talk about what they see on each page, and to look for interesting pictures and words they know. English language learners paired with experienced English speakers will benefit from the low-risk context for using language to name objects, discuss illustrations, and share their interests.

Modeled Writing with an Emphasis on Letters

Modeled writing is a teacher-led instructional technique that involves making explicit a planned set of key concepts. The focus of this lesson is on *letter recognition*. Depending on need, modeled writing lessons may be implemented with the whole class or small groups.

1. Select a purpose for writing that will be meaningful to the participating students. For example, you may write a note, a list, or a sentence about something the class has observed or experienced.

2. As the group observes, use chart paper or a whiteboard to model the writing. As you write, place an emphasis on the names of the letters. For example, "*Dear* . . . That starts with a *D*. This is the letter *D*. Watch me write it." Show students where the letters can be found on large alphabet strips posted in the classroom. To keep more advanced students appropriately challenged, also emphasize letter-sound relationships. Provide a copy of the modeled writing for all participating students to read and reread.

3. Follow up the modeled writing lesson by providing opportunities for students to do their own writing. Work closely with students who need support finding letters on the alphabet strip or remembering how to form the letters.

Shared Writing with an Emphasis on Letters

Writing of any type is a key way to facilitate students' entry into reading. *Shared writing* is a teacher-led instructional technique that involves the teacher and students sharing the pen to explore a planned set of key concepts. The focus of this lesson is on *letter recognition and formation*. Depending on need, it may be used with small groups or the whole class.

1. Select a purpose for writing that will be meaningful to the participating students. For example, you may write a note, a list, or a sentence about something the class has observed or experienced.

2. As the whole group observes, use chart paper or a whiteboard to share the responsibility of the writing. Allow students to write some of the letters for you, and support them when they are unsure how to form the letters. More advanced students will be appropriately challenged if you encourage them to consider letter-sound relationships as part of the writing, and less advanced students will also benefit from this process. Provide a copy of the shared writing for all participating students to read and reread.

3. Follow up by providing opportunities for students to do their own writing. Work closely with students who need support finding letters on the alphabet strip or remembering how to form the letters.

Scaffolded Writing

When students receive support with their writing, they develop a broad range of knowledge that feeds their reading. *Scaffolded writing* is a child-centered experience in which students write in small teacher-supported groups as the teacher observes and provides individualized support. The teacher support can focus on conventions, organization, or ideas. As they write, students are encouraged to talk, share ideas, and help one another. To make the writing feel manageable for students who are hesitant or lack confidence, you may assign them to start by drawing and labeling what they have drawn.

Name Cards

The *name card* lesson uses familiar words (names) to support children's development of letter knowledge. Depending on need, it may be implemented with the whole class or with small groups of students who need to work on recognizing and forming letters.

1. Prepare a name card for each child participating in the lesson. Make a name card with your own name on it to use for modeling.

2. Hand out the name cards to the appropriate owners. Show your own name card and ask the children to observe as you point to or trace each letter. Invite them to do the same with their own name cards. Be sure to use the term *letter* often, because children often confuse this term with *number* and *word*.

3. Ask the children to say each letter in their names to a partner. Then, partners should trade cards and name letters again. Instruct the teams to skip letters that they do not know, or to cover any unknown letters with highlighting tape. (If this activity is implemented in a small group, you can help with naming the letters.) Ask the children to determine if the two names have any of the same letters.

4. Tell the children that you are going to collect the cards and give them back to the wrong person. The students are to talk with each other about the letters and names to see if they can all help one another get their own names back. Implement this step a few times.

5. Repeat this lesson as many times as is helpful. Follow-up lessons may involve categorizing written names by their beginning letters, beginning sounds, number of syllables, or number of letters. Also, have the name cards available to students as they are writing and working on projects during the day.

Word Cards

The *word card* lesson is designed to support letter and word recognition. Depending on who needs this type of support, the lesson may be implemented with the whole class or with small groups of students.

1. Prepare a word card for each child participating in the lesson. Put a different word on each card. You may wish to laminate, as the same set of cards is used for several lessons. You may choose commonly used words, words from your literacy curriculum, or words that are part of a theme or subject your class is studying.

2. Hand out one card to each child, showing the class each word and drawing attention to the sound(s) of the first letter or letters. (The goal is for the students to attempt to read the words on their own.) Keep a card to use for modeling.

3. Model how to use the letters to predict and read the word. For example, "We're using our insect cards today. Mine starts with *A*. Let me think of some insect words that start with *A*. Could this be *ant*? Let me look at the rest of the letters."

4. Instruct students to work with a partner to point at and read the words. Encourage them to look at the first letters first, but also to consider all of the letters in the words.

5. Tell the students that you have a challenge for the partner teams. Ask them to show one of their words to the class and tell about it. Depending on their ability, they may be encouraged to identify some of the letters, all of the letters, the first sound, or the word itself. If you are using content-area words, they could tell something about the meaning of the word. Model the possibilities with your own word card and then ask students to prepare with their partner.

6. Allow several students to respond, prompting as it is helpful.

7. As a follow-up, the cards may be placed in a word study center. Encourage students to sort them in various ways and read the letters or words to one another. Also have the cards available to students as they are writing and working on related projects throughout the day.

Structured Letter Play

Structured letter play is a student-centered experience that offers children the opportunity to talk and share information about letters in a collaborative and purposeful context.

1. Have available enough magnetic letters or letter tiles for children to use in small groups or at a center.

2. On different days, assign the following activities to students. You can differentiate by assigning different activities to different students.

   • Name as many letters as you can. Sort into piles of letters you can and cannot name. Select one letter from the unknown pile and find out its name. Trace the letter and picture it in your mind. Write it on a sticky note and take it home.

   • Make your names.

   • Make words.

   • Make words from the word wall.

   • Make three-letter words.

   • Make four-letter words.

   • Put the letters in ABC order.

   • Make color words (post a list).

   • Make number words (post a list).

- Make words from a unit of study (post a list).

- Sort the letters into uppercase and lowercase piles.

- Match uppercase and lowercase letters.

- Separate the consonants and vowels.

Manipulating Letters

Manipulating letters is a student-centered experience that offers a multimodal, nonthreatening way to experiment with forming letters. Depending on need, it may be implemented in centers, in small groups, or with the whole class and can be embedded into small-group guided reading sessions under *language study.* (See pages 219–220 and 233–234.)

1. Have available a set of trays containing either play dough or sand.

2. Show the students how to use the material to form letters. As you are modeling, encourage students to suggest words for you to form. Show how you can copy different words from around the room.

3. Set up a center for children to use the material to write letters and words or arrange for the whole class to participate in this activity as they sit together in groups.

4. If you are working with small groups, use the Letter and Sound Assessment (Part 1) to select the letters students should practice.

Alphabet Strips

Many children have access to alphabet strips in the classroom, but have little idea how to use them to support their writing. The *alphabet strip* lesson is a whole-class experience designed to show students the various ways they can use alphabet strips as a tool to support their writing.

1. Have available an alphabet strip for each child. (See page 182.) The strips may be taped to tables or desks, or they may be laminated and stored in a large envelope.

2. Lead the students to point to each letter on the strip while saying or singing the letters of the alphabet.

3. Ask the students to look at the pictures and name each with a partner.

4. Ask the students why a butterfly is pictured under the *B*, and so on with three or four additional letters.

5. Ask the students to find the first letter of their names and identify the picture associated with that letter. Discuss whether the picture and the students' names begin with the same sound.

6. Ask the students how they think the strips could help them as they are writing. (Accept all responses.)

7. Support the students in using the strips as they are writing, as a way to remember what letters look like or to help figure out the sounds the letters make. Have the strips available for students to use while writing throughout the year.

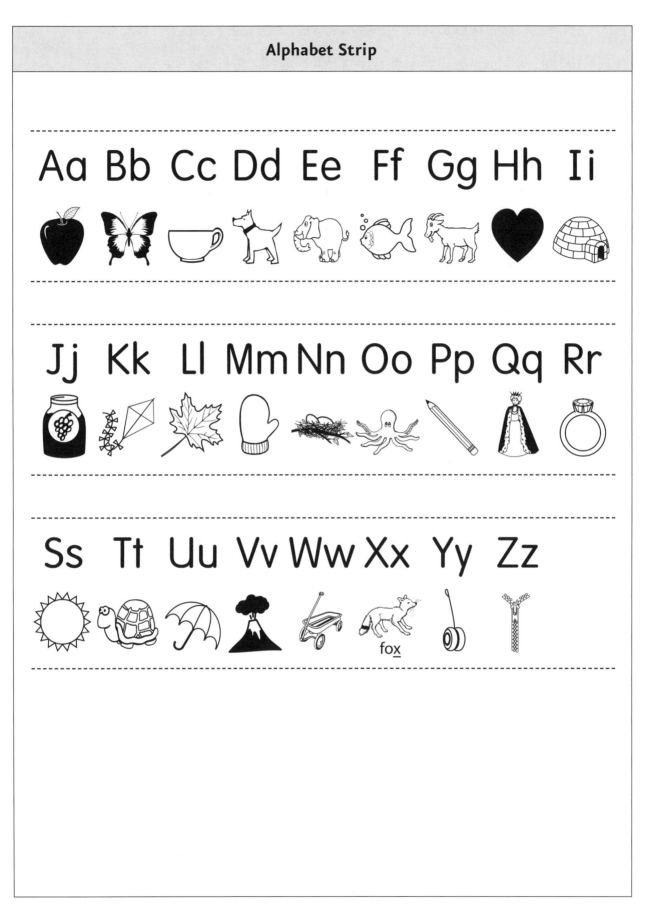

Alphabet Book Study

Alphabet book study is designed to support children in examining the many types of alphabet books, as well as the ways in which alphabet book authors use letters and sounds. The experience begins with the whole class and then moves to centers/teams.

1. Collect a set of alphabet books to share with your students.

2. Read the books to them, highlighting their similarities and differences. With each book, examine how the author has used letters and sounds.

3. Make the books available in a bin or at an alphabet book center.

4. As an optional follow-up, create a class alphabet book that involves each child in creating one page. You can differentiate by encouraging some students to draw a picture and work out the spelling for one word while others can draw and work out spelling for an entire sentence or more.

Alphabet Mat Activities

Alphabet mat activities can be differentiated to allow students to explore letters or sounds. Depending on your students' needs, they can support students in learning to identify letters or sounds, or match pictures with beginning sounds. Alphabet mat activities can be done with small groups, with teams of two, or in centers. To get started, prepare for each participating student a laminated alphabet mat (page 185) and a bag of laminated letter tiles (see page 186). Students may engage in the following experiences.

* Students point to each letter while singing the alphabet song or saying the alphabet. The goal is to maintain one-to-one correspondence. This activity can also be implemented with an audiotape of the alphabet being named or sung.

* Students work together to place letters (lowercase) along the mat to match with the uppercase letters.

* Students work together to say the sound that each letter makes.

* Students are instructed (either by the teacher, a volunteer, or an audio-recorded message) to "Point to the *D*. Check with a partner. Point to the *T*. Check with a partner."

- Students are instructed (either by the teacher, a volunteer, or an audio-recorded message) to "Find the *D*. Check it with your partner. Trace the *D*. Trace it in the air. Write it on paper. Find the *S*. Check it with your partner. Trace the *S*. Trace it in the air. Write it on paper."

- Students are given small pictures (page 187) to place along the mat, matching the object (beginning sound) to the appropriate letter. For example, a *violin* is placed on the *V*. Students work together to check their work.

- Teams choose six to eight letters on the mat and find the matching picture. For each chosen letter, they write the word.

Be sure to use your assessments to hone in on the specific letters and sounds students need to work with. The experience should be challenging but achievable for all who participate.

Alphabet Mat			
A	B	C	D
E	F	G	H
I	J	K	L
M	N	O	P
Q	R	S	T
U	V	W	X
Y	Z		

© 2010 by Gretchen Owocki, from *The RTI Daily Planning Book, K–6*. Portsmouth, NH: Heinemann.

a	b	c	d
e	f	g	h
i	j	k	l
m	n	o	p
q	r	s	t
u	v	w	x
y	z		

Pictures for Alphabet Mat

For Students Needing Support Developing Phonological Awareness

Oral Language Study

Oral language study can be used to explore a number of literacy concepts and is an important part of the classroom day, especially for English language learners. Depending on need, it can be implemented with small groups or the whole class, and it can be used to teach concepts ranging from vocabulary and academic language to phonics and word analysis. When the emphasis is on *phonological awareness*, the instruction involves teaching students to segment and blend word parts and sounds. Children can develop this competency by playing around with oral language, playing around with written language, and combining their explorations of the two.

To implement oral language study with a focus on phonological awareness, set aside five to ten minutes per day (or time during small-group work) to read aloud poetry, nursery rhymes, songs, and jump rope rhymes, orally highlighting and discussing with children the rhyming or alliterative words. Tapping or clapping along will help students to notice and attend to the syllables (White 2008). Repeat the rhymes often throughout the day so they become part of a growing repertoire of known verses. Knowing rhymes *orally* helps children to make connections between spoken and written language when they see the rhymes in *print*.

In a review of studies focused on phonemic awareness, the National Reading Panel (2000) found that just five to eighteen hours of teaching can yield very large effects on students' phonemic awareness; that teaching students to segment and blend with actual written letters is more useful than teaching without print; and that older readers who have developed difficulties can benefit from support developing phonemic awareness.

Modeled Writing with an Emphasis on Listening for Sounds

Modeled writing is a teacher-led instructional technique that involves making explicit a planned set of key concepts. In the present lesson, the focus is on teaching children about how words are made up of individual sounds. The lesson integrates phonological awareness and phonics.

1. Select a purpose for writing that will be meaningful to the participating students. For example, you may write a note, a list, or a sentence about something the class has observed or experienced.

2. As the students observe, use chart paper or a whiteboard to model the writing. As you write, model how to stretch words and listen for the sounds.

3. As a follow-up, provide opportunities for students to do their own writing independently or in a small-group/intervention setting, and encourage them to listen for the sounds in words. For students who are unsure of what to write, encourage drawing first and then encourage them to label what they have drawn. For students who are unsure about stretching words, do the stretching for them, and make the sounds obvious.

Scaffolded Spelling (Manyak 2008)

Scaffolded spelling is a teacher-guided instructional technique that supports students in learning to listen for sounds in words. The experience integrates the study of phonological awareness and phonics. Depending on student needs, it may be implemented with the whole class or small groups.

1. Choose three to five words that include letters/sounds the students know or have been taught. Have available a small whiteboard or a half-sheet of paper for each student.

2. One word at a time, ask students to stretch the words and listen for the sounds. Encourage them to use a hand to "stretch the word like bubble gum," as they articulate each phoneme. Then, ask the students to stretch the word again, stopping after the first sound to think about what letter makes that sound. Ask students to stretch the word again, listening for the second sound, writing the letter, and so on.

3. After the words are written, read them together with the children two times.

4. Follow up with small/intervention groups. Scaffolded spelling can be embedded into small-group guided reading lessons under *language study*. (See pages 219–220 and 233–234.) Continue the scaffolding process until students understand how to stretch words and record appropriate sounds.

Object Sorts

Object sorts are a student-centered experience designed to help children learn to listen for the sounds in words. They may be implemented as a center activity in which all students are required to participate or they may be assigned to certain students based on need. If you have English language learners who might not know the names of all the objects, they should work in teams with students who will know the English names.

1. Collect about three or four small metallic buckets and several small objects to place in them. The objects should be collected with the beginning sound in mind. Attach a magnetic letter to each bucket to let students know how to organize the objects. For example, students might have twenty-four small objects (such as a dime, a pig, and a turtle) to place into one of three buckets labeled *D*, *P*, or *T*.

2. Students sort the objects according to initial sounds (onsets). For more advanced students, you may prepare sorts related to medial or vowel sounds, or end sounds.

3. Follow up by continuing the experience with small groups or intervention groups as it is useful. Object sorts can be embedded into small-group guided reading lessons under *language study*. (See pages 219–220 and 233–234.) Provide extensive modeling and time for discussion.

Onset-Rime Lessons (Caldwell and Leslie 2009)

In *onset-rime lessons*, students are guided to explore the segmenting and blending of written onset and rime parts. The lessons integrate the study of phonological awareness and phonics. Depending on which students need support in these areas, the instruction may occur with the whole class or small groups and can be embedded into small-group guided reading sessions under *language study*. (See pages 219–220 and 233–234.)

1. Have available six to eight printed onsets and one rime that can be moved around (see pages 192 and 193). Be sure that all of the participating students can see the materials from where they will be sitting. If working with the whole class, you can attach Velcro to the back of each piece and use a felt board for display.

2. Tell the students that you will be blending word parts together. Show them the first parts (onsets) to be blended into the one rime. You say the onset (as in *fl-*) and have the students say the rime (as in *-ame*). Then, ask them to blend the onset and rime to make a word (*flame*). Work through several different onsets, keeping the same rime. Provide teams or groups with their own onset-rime sets to work through. To differentiate, give beginners several onsets and one rime. More advanced students can work with a mix.

3. Follow up with small groups/intervention groups as it is appropriate. Continue the lesson with onsets and rimes that have proven difficult for the students.

Common Onsets

b	c	d	f	g
h	j	k	l	m
n	p	qu	r	s
t	v	w	x	y
z	br	cr	dr	fr
gr	pr	tr	wr	bl
cl	fl	gl	pl	sl
sc	sk	sm	sn	sp
st	sw	ch	sh	th
wh				

Thirty-seven Most Common Rimes				
ack	all	ain	ake	ale
ame	an	ank	ap	ask
at	ate	aw	ay	eat
ell	est	ice	ick	ide
ight	ill	in	ine	ing
ink	ip	ir	ock	oke
op	or	ore	uck	ug
ump	unk			

From Wylie and Durrell (1970)

Rhyme Lessons (Caldwell and Leslie 2009)

Rhyme lessons are designed to support students in learning to blend word parts. The lessons may be implemented with the whole class or in small, needs-based groups and can be embedded into small-group guided reading sessions under *language study*. (See pages 219–220 and 233–234.)

1. Post the alphabet in the classroom, or have an alphabet strip for each child/group to use (see page 182). Select a common rime from page 193 and write it at the top of a piece of chart paper.

2. Starting at the beginning of the alphabet, model how to try out a consonant as an onset for the rime (word part). The goal is to find real words. For example, if the chosen rime is *-ame*, show the students how to blend /b/ with *-ame*, and then determine if a real word has been created. Model with a few consonants, until you have located at least one real word and one nonword. Point out to students that all of the words rhyme.

3. Place the students in pairs or groups to locate other real words that rhyme with the one you have identified so far. Students record their words on note cards. Students may keep these words as part of a personal word bank or to use for future activities.

4. Have each pair or group share a word they made. Over time, repeat the lesson with different rimes.

5. Follow up with small groups/intervention groups as appropriate. This lesson may be continued over time until students demonstrate competency segmenting and blending.

Sound Boxes (McCarthy 2008/2009)

Sound boxes are used to support children in learning how to segment and blend word parts. Depending on need, they may be implemented with individuals or small groups and can be embedded into small-group guided reading lessons under *language study*. (See pages 219–220 and 233–234.)

1. To prepare for the lesson, copy and laminate several sound cards (pages 196–201), or make your own cards. The cards should contain a picture of a one-syllable word at the top, a box for each sound in

the word in the middle, and a blank space for markers at the bottom. Choose pictures of familiar, one-syllable words with sounds that can be distinctly heard.

Some recommended words by level of difficulty:

Words without blends: *bike, can, cup, dog, duck, fish, five, leaf, map, net, pan, sun*

Words with blends: *block, broom, brush, frog, grass, hand, sled, spoon, stop, swim, train, truck*

2. Model how to stretch words into their phonemes, and demonstrate how to push a marker into one of the boxes for each phoneme articulated. For example: "Bag. /b/ /a/ /g/."

3. Give each student a sound box card. Stretch the word as students push the markers into the boxes, and then you push the markers as students stretch the words.

4. Help students stretch and push independently.

5. Follow up with small groups and intervention groups as appropriate. This lesson may be continued over time, until students demonstrate competency with segmenting and blending.

Sound Boxes with Pictures

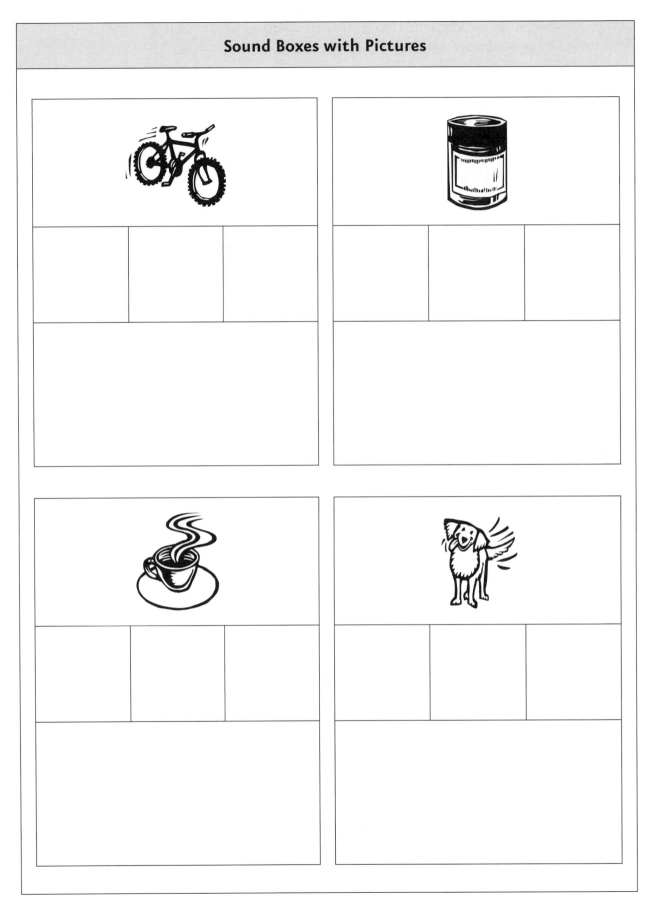

Sound Boxes with Pictures

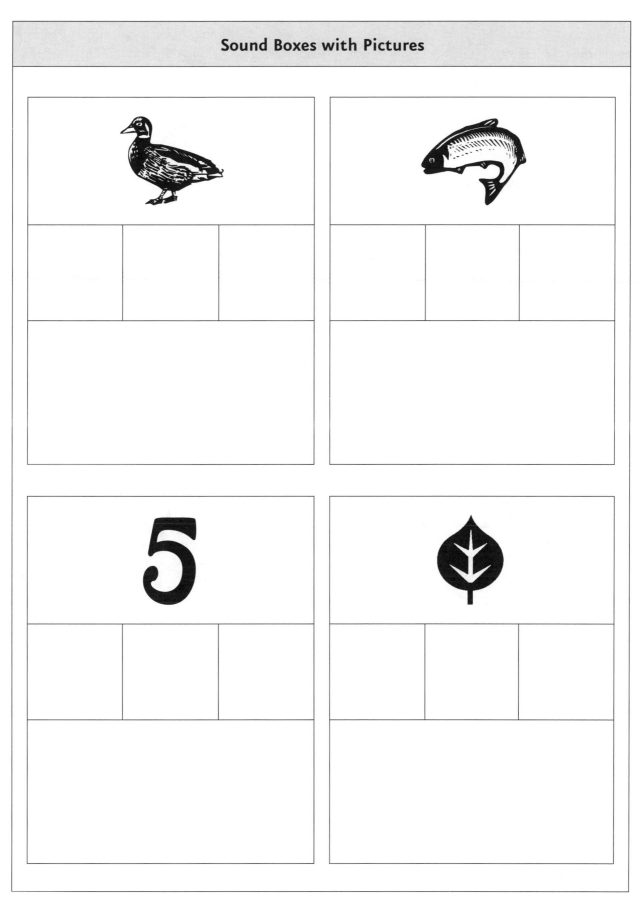

Sound Boxes with Pictures

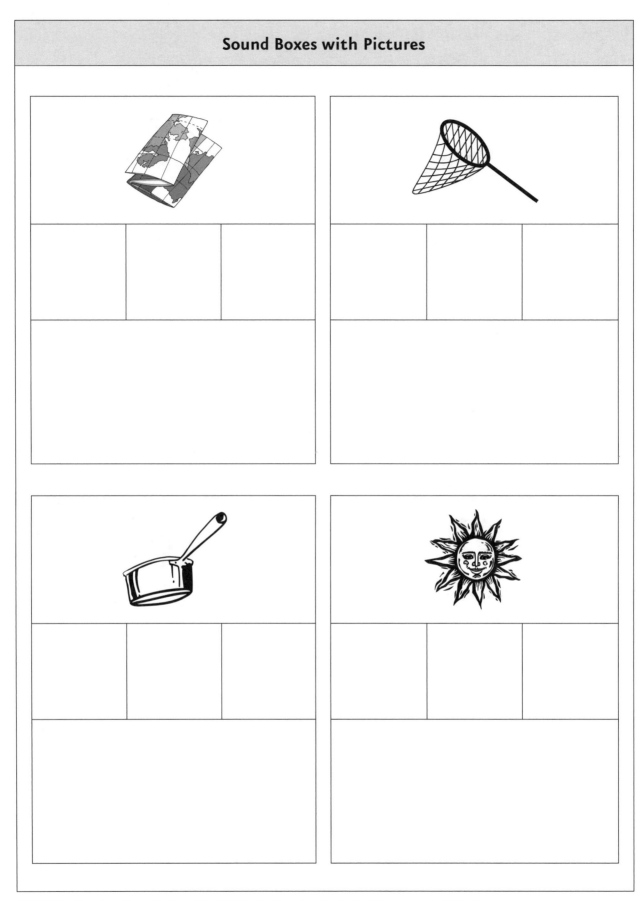

Sound Boxes with Pictures

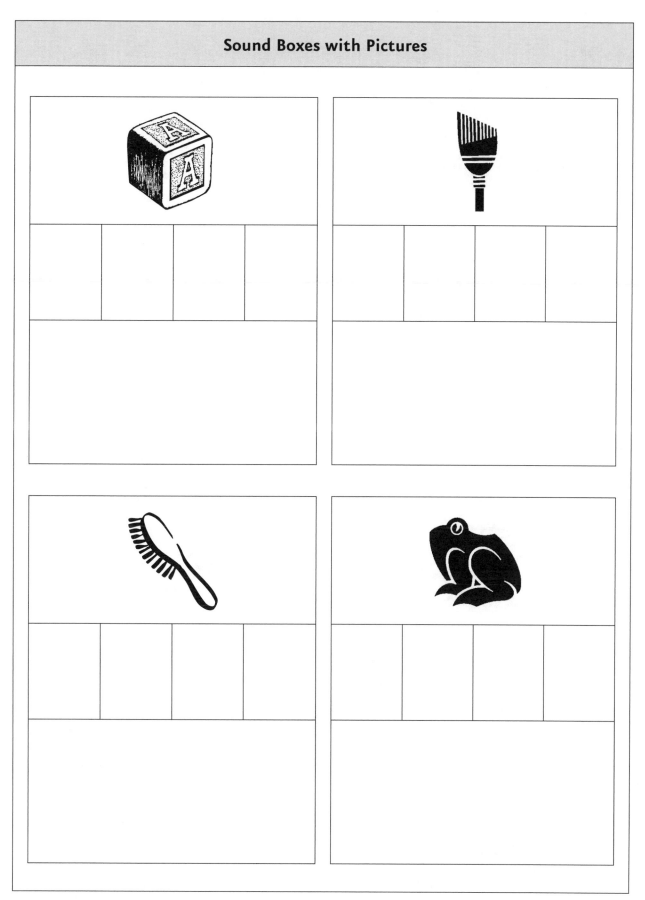

Sound Boxes with Pictures

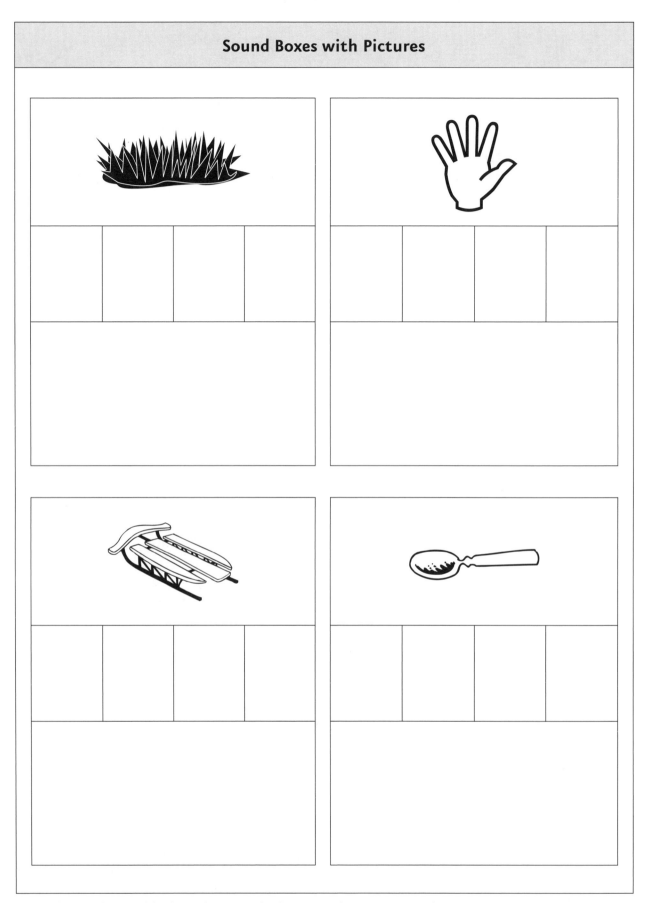

Sound Boxes with Pictures

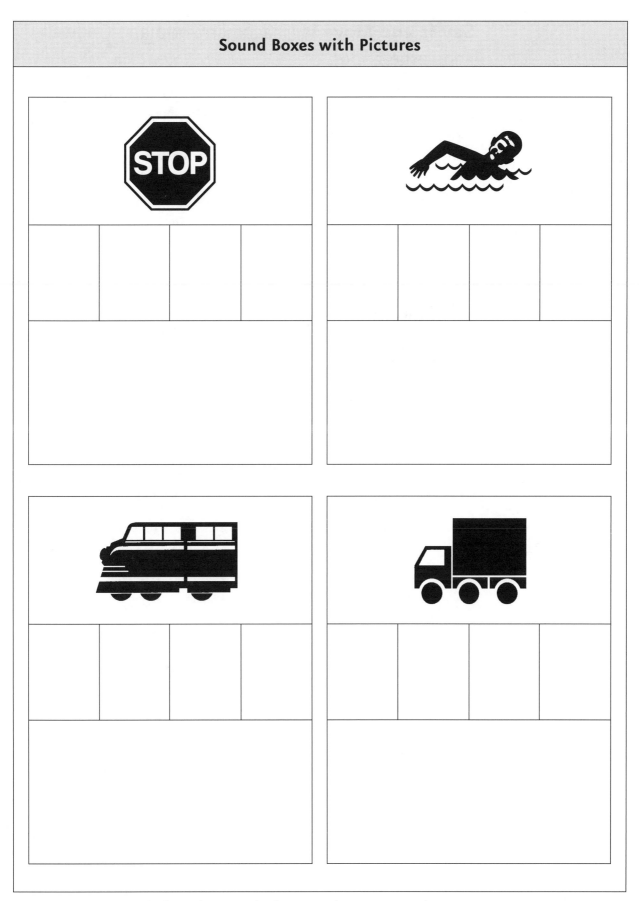

Say It and Move It (Blachman 2000 and Caldwell and Leslie 2009)

Say It and Move It is a small-group strategy designed for students learning to segment and blend and can be embedded into small-group guided reading sessions under *language study*. (See pages 219–220 and 233–234.) The strategy merges the study of phonological awareness and phonics.

1. Give each participating student a paper with four sound boxes (page 196), and a small set of letter cards or tiles, such as *a, b, e, f, m, t* (page 186).

2. Say a word with two, three, or four phonemes and help students to say the individual phonemes in the word as they push the corresponding letter into the boxes. For example, "Bat. /b/ /a/ /t/."

3. Encourage students to run a finger under the letters as they blend the sounds together to make a word.

4. Repeat the process until the students have worked for approximately five minutes. Example set: *at, bat, fat, mat, met, bet.*

5. Follow up with small groups and intervention groups as appropriate. This lesson may be continued over time, until students demonstrate competency with segmenting and blending.

Sound Box Mat			

For Students Needing Support Developing Phonics Knowledge and Word Analysis

Word Study

Word study is a practice designed to support children's development of understandings about letters, letter-sound relationships, words, and patterns in words. The focus of this word study lesson is on developing phonics knowledge and word analysis skill. With appropriate differentiation, all students in your classroom are likely to benefit. The following procedures may be implemented throughout the school year, in small groups or with the whole class. It is recommended that they be embedded into the *language study* phase of guided reading lessons. (See pages 219–220 and 233–234.)

1. Have available a whiteboard or sheet of chart paper for recording words. Place students in teams of two. Each team will need a small whiteboard and a marker.

2. Select a focus word to get the study started. It is recommended that you select based on words or parts that have presented difficulty to this group of students (see pages 192 and 193); you may also select words (or parts) that several students are using frequently in their writing but spelling incorrectly or miscuing on frequently; or multisyllabic words in general. The High-Frequency Word Inventory (Part 1), the Spelling Inventory (Part 1), and the Reading Assessment (Part 1) can help you to make selections based on students' demonstrated needs.

3. Write the focus word on the chart paper and ask students what they notice. For example:

    * What is this word?

    * Have you seen it before?

    * Have you used it in your writing?

    * What sounds do the letters make?

    * Does it have any special features (such as digraphs, blends, long vowel patterns, or double consonants)?

    * Name some words that rhyme.

- Can you name other words with the same onset/rime/affixes?

- What is in the middle of the word?

4. Cover the word and ask the partners to think about the spelling as each takes a turn writing it down. Then allow them to check their work.

5. Ask the partners to write as many words as they can with the same onset, rime, prefix, suffix, or root.

6. Record contributions from volunteers on the chart paper, making different columns of words as appropriate. For example, if you are studying the rime *-ain* and students suggest *cane*, talk about the different spellings, and start a new column for *-ane* words.

7. Repeat this process often with different words and word parts. The lesson format may be shared between the whole class, small groups, and intervention groups.

Word Sorts

Word sorts are student-centered small-group activities designed to help students to develop their phonics and word knowledge. They involve students in using prepared cards to sort and study words. Blank cards are also provided for students to make their own materials. Great care should be taken to determine the types of sorts that students actually need. The High-Frequency Word Inventory (Part 1), the Spelling Inventory (Part 1), the Letter and Sound Assessment (Part 1), and the Reading Assessment (Part 1) can help you to make selections based on students' demonstrated needs.

Onsets: Sort word cards by onsets (for example, *l-*, *tr-*, *ch-*). Read the words. Write some words to add to the stack.

Rimes/rhymes: Sort the word cards by rimes or rhymes (for example, *-ate*, *-ash*, *-at* or *bear*, *care*, *hair*). Read the words. Write some words to add to the stack.

Multisyllabic words: Sort the word cards by affixes. Read the words. Write some words to add to the stack.

Number of letters: Sort the word cards into piles according to the number of letters they contain. Read each pile. Write a word to add to each stack.

Vowel sounds: Sort the word cards into piles according to the sound that their vowels make. Write a word to add to each stack.

Alphabetical order: Place the cards in alphabetical order.

Student-Made Alphabet Books

Alphabet books create a rich forum for studying letters, sounds, and words. Arrange for the class to create an alphabet book using writing and drawing. You may require that students follow a theme (animals, families, forces). Each child contributes one page. To vary the level of difficulty, individual children may be assigned to write one word, an entire sentence, or more than one sentence on the page. Place the finished book in a reading center or the class library.

Word Hunts

Word hunts involve students in moving throughout the classroom or through stacks of books, hunting for words, talking about their makeup, and recording them on clipboards. To implement, prepare several strips of paper with one hunt per strip (see below for examples). Send the students off in teams. When students hunt words in books, previously read books should be used. Make available baskets of familiar books to serve this purpose.

You can differentiate by sending students on different types of word hunts. For example, some students might be required to find, record, and read five words that begin with *B* (relatively simple), while others might be required to find, record, and read five words with more than eight letters (relatively complex). A Spelling Inventory (Part 1) and samples of student writing can be used to develop hunts that will be challenging but achievable. Following is a starter list of word hunts:

- Find five words that you can read.

- Find five words that start with ___.

- Find five words to take home and read to a family member.

- Find a word beginning with each letter of the alphabet.

- Find five words that you would like to remember how to spell.

- Find three words that start like *quack*.

- Find three words that end with *ing*.

- Find five words that end with *ed*.

- Find five words in their plural form.

- Find five past-tense words.

- Find three compound words.

- Find two words that rhyme with *fox*.

- Find five contractions.

- Find five words with only one or two letters.

- Find three words with more than eight letters.

- Find five first names.

- Find the two shortest and two longest last names in our class.

- Find three words that have a spelling pattern like *grape*, *game*, *have*, and *tape*.

- Find three words that start with vowels.

Word Challenges

Word challenges involve children in teams working to analyze words and their parts. Students may be challenged to do the following:

- *Put together and read cut-apart two-, three-, and four-letter words.* Store each word in a separate envelope. To help keep the pieces organized, number the envelopes, and put the same number on the back of each letter that goes in that envelope. Students move around the letters until they have made a word. To differentiate, color-code the envelopes so that you know which are easier and which are harder.

- *Make two-, three-, and four-letter words from a longer base word.* For example, starting with the word *motion*, students can make a list that includes *to, in, on, moon, no, not,* and *tin*.

Word Building

Word building is a teacher-led small-group experience designed to help children develop letter, sound, and word knowledge. The experience is highly adaptable to meet different levels of knowledge and can be embedded into small-group guided reading sessions in the *language study* phase of the lesson. (See pages 219–220 and 233–234.)

1. Have available magnetic letters or letter tiles for students to use for building words.

2. Start by naming a series of two-letter words, and progress from there. For example, using the letters *A, E, I, B, C, F, K, S,* and *T,* students might be instructed to build these words: *it, at, cat, bat, fat, fit, bit, bite, kite, kites.* Elevate the complexity of the words to the point that what you are asking children to do is challenging but achievable. Work on parts that reflect demonstrated needs.

Scaffolded Writing

Scaffolded writing is a child-centered experience in which students write in teacher-supported small groups. As students are writing, the teacher makes a point to provide support with spelling, helping students stretch words and listen for their sounds, think about known patterns, and use the word wall and other print resources as supports for their spelling. For students who are just moving into stretching words, you may support them by having them write the first letter of the word, and you can write or help with the rest. The knowledge students develop through writing will support their development as readers.

For Students Needing Support Decoding Multisyllabic Words

Syllable and Part Blending

Syllable and part-blending activities support students in developing familiarity with common word parts and in learning to deal flexibly with parts by trying out more than one sound if the first attempt does not work. Depending on need, these activities can be done with small groups or the whole class, and can be embedded into guided reading sessions in the *language study* phase of the lesson. (See pages 219–220 and 233–234.)

1. Have available multisyllabic words on strips of paper, cut apart by syllable. Choose the words from the content-area texts or other literature your students are reading. (See page 210 for a starter set of words to use.)

2. If you are working with the whole class, place students in groups.

3. Give each group three to five cut-up words (all mixed together). As a team, the groups put the syllables together until they have formed a complete set of multisyllabic words. To vary the difficulty, less experienced students can be given two-syllable words to work with at first.

Multisyllabic Words

Most multisyllabic words have at least one prefix or suffix. Being able to identify these, and pull them apart from the root of the word, makes the decoding more manageable and is much more efficient than attempting to move through a word sound by sound. In addition to teaching students to break words into parts, it is also helpful to teach them to be "flexible" with identifying word parts. If one attempt at a vowel sound doesn't work, then another sound should be tried. Children begin to know words and parts automatically as a result of encountering them several times (Calhoun and Leslie 2002) and working through their pronunciations (Ehri 1998).

Blending Syllables and Parts

mag	net	ic		in	ter	fer	ence
re	con	struct		ex	per	i	ment
im	per	fect		trans	por	ta	tion
ex	pan	sion		car	bo	hy	drate
de	vel	op		ap	prox	i	mate
pre	vent	ing		con	tin	ent	al
un	fold	ed		in	tel	li	gent
in	ter	rupt		en	er	get	ic
con	tain	er		pre	dom	in	ate
star	va	tion		con	tam	in	ate
tri	umph	ant		sci	en	tif	ic
mas	ter	ful		pre	his	tor	ic
in	stru	ment		de	lib	er	ate
cir	cum	stance		com	plex	i	ty
sud	den	ly		pop	u	la	tion
me	te	or		mal	nu	tri	tion
qui	et	ly		min	er	al	ize
as	tro	naut		re	la	tion	ship
nu	tri	ent		con	ser	va	tion

Parts Analysis

Parts analysis activities support students who need to learn to segment and blend multisyllabic words. This activity is implemented with small groups and can be embedded into your guided reading sessions in the *language study* phase of the lesson. (See pages 219–220 and 233–234.)

1. Collect three or four multisyllabic words that have presented difficulty for students. You will be working with one word at a time.

2. Students copy the challenging word.

    Examples: *expansion, continuous*

3. Students identify any prefixes and suffixes/endings and write them separately from the base word or middle part of the word.

    Examples: *ex-pan-sion, con-tinu-ous*

4. Students divide the base word or remaining part of the word into pronounceable parts by inserting a slash mark as needed. Encourage flexibility. For example, if a long vowel sound doesn't work, encourage the student to attempt a short vowel sound. Then, students blend the parts of the word to read it aloud.

    Examples: *ex-pan-sion, con-tin-u-ous*

Spelling in Parts (Powell and Aram 2008)

Spelling in parts is a strategy that helps students learn to focus on spelling patterns and learn to break multisyllabic words into chunks. Depending on needs, it can be implemented with small groups or the whole class and can be embedded into your small-group/intervention guided reading sessions in the language study phase of the lesson. (See pages 219–220 and 233–234.)

1. Have available a short list of multisyllabic words from the texts students are reading or be prepared to ask students to suggest words from the content areas they are studying.

2. Looking at one word, the teacher reads it, then students repeat the word slowly, clapping once for each syllable. (Check to see that the division is reasonable; this can be done without teaching the specific rules for dividing words into syllables.)

3. Students say the syllables one at a time, writing the spelling of each on a whiteboard or paper. With teacher guidance, they circle and discuss syllables that have difficult spelling patterns.

4. Students cover or erase the word and write it independently, saying each syllable before writing it.

Tricky Passages (Manning, Chumley, and Underbakke 2006)

Tricky passage lessons are implemented in small groups and can be embedded into your guided reading sessions in the *language study* phase of the lesson. (See pages 219–220 and 233–234.) Tricky passage lessons are designed to support students in reading multisyllabic words in context.

1. Select a passage containing numerous multisyllabic words. Discuss the importance of these words. Have the students highlight the words or cover them with colored tape to consider their prevalence.

2. Think aloud about the strategies you use to read and understand multisyllabic words (look for known chunks, cover chunks to see if meaningful parts can be found, skip and go back to make a prediction).

3. Have the students read the passage silently, trying out the strategies. Ask them to mark any unknown multisyllabic words. Then, have them take turns reading sections of the passage aloud. They should help one another, sharing the strategies they used and working together to decode any unknown words.

Word Recording

Word recording takes place during independent reading. Students place a sticky note on the cover of the book they are reading. When they come to a multisyllabic word they are unable to solve, the students record the word on the sticky note, including the page number.

When the students meet with the teacher in small groups, the collected words are used for strategy instruction.

For Students Needing Support Reading High-Frequency Words

Word Study and Word Wall

Word study is a practice designed to support children's development of understandings about letter-sound relationships, words, and patterns in words. This word study lesson is designed to support students who need to develop their repertoire of *high-frequency* words or parts. The procedures may be implemented throughout the school year, in small groups or with the whole class, and can be embedded into your guided reading sessions in the *language study* phase of the lesson. (See pages 219–220 and 233–234.)

1. Have available a whiteboard or sheet of chart paper for recording words. Place students in teams of two. Each team will need a small whiteboard and marker.

2. Select a high-frequency *focus word* or a high-frequency word part. It is recommended that you select words that have proven difficult for this group of students. Write the focus word on the chart paper and ask students what they notice. For example:

   - What is this word? Have you seen it before?

   - Count the number of letters.

   - Talk about the sounds the letters make.

   - Name (or write) words with the same onsets.

   - Name (or write) words with the same rimes.

   - Does the word have any special features (such as digraphs, blends, long vowel patterns, or double consonants)?

3. Tell students to look closely at the word because you are going to cover it and ask them to spell it. After a volunteer spells it, uncover the word to check the spelling.

4. Ask each partner to write the word and check their spelling.

5. Repeat the process with one to three additional words. Place the studied words on a word wall.

6. Check your student's knowledge the next day, asking them to write the studied words from memory. Encourage them to use the word wall to support their writing.

7. Repeat this process often with different words and word parts. The lesson format may be shared between the whole class, small groups, and intervention groups. To focus on words or parts that have proven difficult, use the High-Frequency Word Inventory (Part 1), the Spelling Inventory (Part 1), or the Reading Assessment (Part 1).

Visual-Auditory-Kinesthetic-Tactile Approach

The *visual-auditory-kinesthetic-tactile* (VAKT) approach was originated by the work of Grace Fernald and adapted by many. VAKT makes use of varied modalities. It is implemented in small groups with students who need to develop word-level knowledge and can be embedded into your small-group/ intervention guided reading sessions in the *language study* phase of the lesson. (See pages 219–220 and 233–234.)

1. Students choose one to three words they need to practice for fluency. You can use a high-frequency word inventory to help students identify the words.

2. Students observe as you say their chosen words while writing them with a crayon or other writing utensil that provides texture.

3. Students say their words while tracing them with a finger.

4. Students write the words from memory.

Manipulating Words

Manipulating words is a student-centered experience that offers a nonthreatening way to explore the makeup of words. It can be used to teach high-frequency words as well as word parts or families. The activity is implemented with small groups and can be embedded into small-group guided reading lessons under *language study*. (See pages 219–220 and 233–234.)

1. Choose one to three words each student needs to practice for fluency. You can use a high-frequency word inventory to help identify the words.

2. Provide students with small trays containing a layer of salt. Students use a Q-tip to write high-frequency words. They check their work with a partner. To individualize, different students can write different words, based on demonstrated needs.

Transparency Tape Lists

Transparency tape lists provide a visual way for students to monitor their progress as they learn new words. The strategy is implemented with one student at a time, but groups can work together for the follow-up word study.

1. Test students informally as they read a high-frequency word list (see Part 1). Each word read correctly is covered with a piece of colored, transparent tape. Unknown words are left without tape.

2. Have the student take the list home to practice, and provide varied types of word instruction in the classroom.

3. Test again, using a different color of tape to cover the known words.

4. Continue the cycle.

Word Concentration

Word concentration is played as a center or small-group activity, as a way to practice reading high-frequency words.

1. Prepare twenty-four cards (twelve written words to match twelve identical written words, or twelve pictures to match twelve words).

2. Show students how to lay the cards out so the words and pictures cannot be seen. Students take turns turning over two at a time to find matches.

Retrospective Miscue Analysis: High-Frequency Words

Retrospective Miscue Analysis (RMA) (Goodman and Marek 1996) is a small-group instructional tool that helps students to become consciously aware of their reading knowledge and strategies. RMA can be used as a way to explore the high-frequency words that are presenting a challenge and can be nested into the work of guided reading groups.

1. Listen to readers and document their miscues on a typewritten copy of the text.

2. Show the students the documented miscues and work together to decode them. Work with the student to look for any miscued words that show up frequently in text and to highlight those words if they do not easily read them during the analysis.

3. Have the students read the words again, within the context of their sentences.

4. As an option, have the students write the words on three-by-five-inch note cards and keep a personal word bank.

Guided Reading

Guided reading is a small-group instructional strategy that can provide students with broad-ranging instruction in the area of text processing and text comprehending. This lesson (see pages 219–220) is designed to emphasize text processing, while the lesson format featured on pages 233–234 is designed to emphasize text comprehension. It is important to keep in mind that even when text processing is the focus, rich discussions about content should take high priority. Without engagement, students will find little reason to read and push themselves to solve problems.

In the present lesson, students read aloud as you document miscues and provide strategy instruction in relation to word analysis and the integrated use of cue systems. The text should be at the instructional level. The Reading Assessment may be used to determine approximate levels of text to use for guided reading instruction, as well as identifying particular areas of text-processing need.

To provide well-tailored text-processing instruction, make it a regular practice to document miscues, and to look for patterns of error. The following questions can guide your analysis:

- What does the student do when encountering unknown words?

- Is there a pattern?

- Do the attempts resemble the actual word? How closely?

- Does the student regularly make low-quality miscues that should have been noticed and corrected?

Use your analysis of miscue patterns to provide appropriate support. Depending on what you find from your analyses, prompt students to do the following:

- Look at the illustrations.

- Look at the word. Let's try it.

- Think about what would make sense.

- Think about what would sound right. (This cue may not be helpful for English language learners.)

- Say the first sound and then read on. Go back to the word.

- Stop and think about punctuation and how the sentence is organized.

Page 219 features a generic lesson plan to use for guided reading with a focus on text processing. The form should be used for observation and joint planning between the classroom teacher and the intervention teacher, and the observations should be discussed regularly in order to inform continued planning. The lesson on page 220 provides an adapted plan for English language learners.

RTI Lesson Plan for Small Groups: Focus on Text Processing

Students: _____

Teacher: _____ Date: _____ Time: _____

RTI Lesson Plan for Small Groups: Focus on Text Processing	Observations to Inform Next Lesson
1. Familiar Rereading of Previous Day's Text Each student reads the selection in a soft voice. The teacher documents miscues from one student. **2. Previewing New Text** Students are guided to preview the text or section to be read. _____ Level _____ **3. Reading** Each student reads the selection in a soft voice. The teacher listens to one reader at a time, providing support and documenting miscues. Conversation is prompted and encouraged after reading. **4. Language Study** Students engage in word work/analysis and evaluation of miscues. The focus is on words and parts that have proven difficult for the students as well as any ineffective use of cue systems. Focus for lesson: Words/Parts _____ Cues _____ **5. Writing (Optional)** Students compose a sentence in response to the book just read. They use invented spelling as appropriate. The teacher provides support with spelling and punctuation. *Optional*: The teacher writes each student's sentence on a strip (conventional spelling) and cuts the words apart for students to reassemble. After reading with a partner, the students take the pieces home to reread. **6. Familiar Rereading** Students reread the new text at home or to a partner.	

RTI Lesson Plan for Small Groups: Focus on Text Processing with English Language Learners

Students: _____

Teacher: _____ Date: _____ Time: _____

RTI Lesson Plan for Small Groups: Focus on Text Processing with English Language Learners	Observations to Inform Next Lesson
1. Rereading of Previous Day's Text Each student reads the selection in a soft voice. The teacher documents miscues from one student. **2. Previewing New Text** Students are guided to preview the text or section to be read. The teacher analyzes the text beforehand to identify any potentially confusing words, meanings, sentence structures, or text structures; and draws student attention to these to mediate meaning making. Visuals, use of illustrations, and gestures are encouraged. _____ Level _____ **3. Reading** _Optional_: The teacher reads the text aloud and guides a discussion focused on comprehension and vocabulary. The teacher assesses student understanding and supports comprehension by encouraging retelling and response to open-ended questions. Each student reads the selection in a soft voice. The teacher listens to one reader at a time, providing support and documenting miscues. Conversation is prompted and encouraged. Note: Keep in mind that English language learners may not have sufficient semantic or syntactic knowledge to consistently use prediction as a strategy; may rely on graphophonic cues; and may not yet have the linguistic knowledge to recognize miscues or know how to correct them. **4. Language Study** Students engage in word study and evaluation of miscues. The focus is on words and parts that have proven difficult for the students as well as syntactic and semantic text features. Focus for lesson: Words/Parts _____ Features/Cues _____ **5. Writing (Optional)** Students compose a sentence in response to the book just read. They use invented spelling as appropriate. The teacher provides support with syntax, spelling, and punctuation. _Optional_: The teacher writes each student's sentence on a strip (conventional spelling) and cuts the words apart for students to reassemble. After reading with a partner, the students take the pieces home to reread. **6. Familiar Rereading** Students reread the new text at home or to a partner.	

Informed by Avalos et al. (2007); Cappelini (2005); Hadaway, Vardell, and Young (2004).

Cue System Prompts

Cue system lessons are designed to help students learn a variety of strategies to implement when they encounter unknown words. Such lessons are particularly useful for students who make many low-quality miscues without self-correcting and for students who focus heavily on analyzing words without making use of the other cues in the sentence. The *cue system prompt* lesson may be implemented with individuals, small groups, or the whole class and can be nested into the work of guided reading groups.

1. Have available a text with all but the onset of every seventh word covered (as in leaving visible the *m* in *mermaid*; the *sh* in *ship*; and the *cr* in *creature*).

2. Ask students to predict the partially covered word by using the following prompts.

   * Look at the start of the word. What would make sense? (This encourages use of the semantic and graphophonic cue systems.)

   * Would that sound right? (This encourages use of the syntactic cue system.) English language learners may not have the English language facility to determine whether a sentence sounds right, but will benefit from discussions that highlight syntactic features and how authors use varying text structures.

3. Uncover the rest of the word and ask students to confirm that their prediction is correct. Remind students to use this strategy while reading. Post the prompts in the classroom.

Miscue Investigation (based on Goodman and Marek 1996)

Miscue investigation is an instructional strategy that helps students to consider the importance of focusing on making sense as they read. It is particularly useful for students who make many low-quality miscues without self-correcting. It is generally implemented with small groups and can be nested into the work of guided reading groups.

1. On a transparency machine or whiteboard, project a text passage that shows six to eight documented miscues. An example is provided on page 222. After using this example, it will be helpful to collect a set of such examples from your own students. Always request student

permission to share the miscues with the class, and start the miscue investigation sessions with examples that contain mostly high-quality miscues (the types that do not render sentence structure or meaning insensible). When the group learns to be supportive and seems to have an understanding that miscues often show good thinking, you can begin to work with lower-quality miscues.

Keep in mind that the quality of a miscue must be evaluated with the speaker's dialect and native language in mind. Even proficient readers often change text into their own way of speaking, creating syntactically incorrect sentences. So when children do so, while technically incorrect, they may actually be showing that they are focused on making meaning.

2. Discuss the miscues using the questions in the box below (based on Goodman and Marek 1996). During initial sessions, be prepared to rephrase and modify questions and to provide a lot of prompting and guidance.

3. With intervention or small-group follow-ups, continue to document miscues and help students to stay focused on meaning as they read. Continue miscue investigation lessons as needed.

Example to Use for Miscue Investigations

Questions for Miscue Investigation

1. Does the miscue look like the word?

2. Why do you think the reader made this miscue?

3. Did the miscue affect the reader's understanding?

4. Should the reader have noticed the miscue and done something about it?

Oh   teeny
On my street, everyone lives in houses with tiny yards.

    Trister?   picture
Only Christie Mann has a swimming pool. There's a price

                              Tristers look
to pay for swimming in that pool. Christie looks like the

sweetest little thing. She's really very cute． But, sweet.

          Trister
she is not. Christie knows her stuff.

222

Retrospective Miscue Analysis

RMA (Goodman and Marek 1996) is a small-group instructional tool that helps students to focus on making sense as they process text. RMA is an especially useful strategy for students who lack confidence in reading or who tend to focus on reading words at the expense of meaning making. It is typically implemented with small groups and can be nested into the work of guided reading/intervention groups.

1. Prepare a copy of reading material that the students are likely to find somewhat challenging to decode. You may wish to use the recommended booklist featured in Figure 1–3 and the forms from the Reading Assessment tool in Part 1 (reproducibles can also be printed from PDFs at this book's product page on the Heinemann website).

2. Document miscues on the copy as you listen to students read without aid from you. Listen to several different readers reading the same text in order to bring groups of students together for RMA sessions.

3. Choose a section of the text that contains several miscues. Be prepared with miscues from each reader. Depending on student needs, you may wish to select a particular type of miscue (omissions, insertions, substitutions, punctuation). For students who lack confidence or who see themselves as poor readers, you can build confidence by initially selecting high-quality miscues—the types that do not render the sentence structure or meaning insensible.

4. Discuss the miscues. Following are suggested questions to get RMA sessions started. During initial sessions, be prepared to rephrase and modify questions, and to provide a lot of prompting and guidance. Follow up in small groups/intervention groups as it is useful.

RMA Questions

1. Why do you think you made this miscue?

2. Did it affect your understanding?

3. Did you correct the miscue? Should you have noticed that something was off, and done something about it?

4. Does the miscue look like the word?

Cooperative Controlled Cloze (Goodman, Watson, and Burke 2005)

Cooperative controlled cloze is a useful strategy for students who are hesitant to take risks while reading. These students may demonstrate such hesitancy by pausing at words for long periods of time; omitting words or phrases; and regularly producing nonword substitutions. The lesson can be implemented with small groups or the whole class and can be nested into the work of guided reading/intervention groups. Cloze experiences provide an especially useful medium for studying issues of syntax and linguistic structure with English language learners.

1. Select a passage from a text that will be unfamiliar to your students. Remove every fifth word, leaving intact one or two sentences at the beginning and at the end of the text. For students who show low confidence or are hesitant, use fewer blanks, as this will make the task easier and build strength through success.

2. Instruct students to read the entire passage aloud together and to then go back and supply the missing words. The object is to attempt to supply the word the author actually used. After supplying the words, the team should read the piece again (silently this time) to ensure that all of the sentences make sense.

3. Using examples from the text, discuss with students the knowledge they bring to reading. For example, "How did you know that would make sense?" "What from the text supported your decision?" "Did you ever reread or read on to help you make the decision?" "How can thinking in these ways help you as you are reading on your own?"

Independent Reading

Independent reading should be a daily part of children's instruction and is especially important to the reading development of students who are not reading within target ranges. Independent reading can be planned as a classroom activity or implemented as homework. To organize, set up three or four leveled bins of books and (without drawing attention to the levels) let students know which to choose from. Or provide each student with a set of books to be kept in a bag for personal use. Having a choice of books will provide students with motivation, and having books at their independent levels will help them to firm up word knowledge and develop fluency (Allington 2006). During independent reading, be sure to observe which students engage with the text and which seem to avoid meaningful reading. Students may need continued support to find the right books and to focus enough to learn from and enjoy the experience.

Repeated Reading

Repeated reading is a widely recognized and very helpful way to support fluency, including for English language learners. To implement this practice, arrange for repeated reading of familiar texts to occur any time throughout the day, including homework time. Students may read texts that have been used for small-group instruction or texts you have read aloud. To work toward motivation and extended reading, allow children to choose their favorites.

Echo Reading

Echo reading is a teacher-led strategy designed to support fluency. It is typically used with small groups and can be nested into the work of guided reading/intervention groups.

1. The teacher reads a section of a passage using appropriate phrasing and prosody. Depending on the group, the section could be as short as a sentence or as long as a paragraph.

2. After the teacher completes the section, the students use their own copies of the passage to echo the teacher's reading.

Paired Reading

Paired reading is a student-centered strategy implemented with teams of two. The whole class may participate at the same time, or the activity can occur as students are working in centers. To implement, a more advanced reader is matched with a less advanced reader. The students read a passage aloud together, either at the same time or with the stronger reader going first and the other reader repeating what has been read.

Team Reading

Team reading is a student-centered strategy implemented with teams of two. The whole class may participate at the same time, or the activity can occur as students are working in centers. To implement, match up teams of two students who are reading at approximately the same level. To ensure that the text will not be too difficult to read with fluency, provide different bins of leveled books and let the teams know which bins they may use. Or provide each student with a set of books to be kept in a bag for personal use and instruct the teams to use one of the bagged books. The students take turns reading pages or longer sections.

Computer and Audio-Recorded Reading

Many books are available online or in audio format, and these materials can be used to support fluency. To implement, individuals or small groups are instructed to listen to recorded literature while following along with the print, and then to read the text independently (with the sound off).

Performance Reading

Performance reading is a student-centered strategy implemented with small groups. To implement, students choose engaging, short passages to perform. Because the passages are practiced several times (with teacher support), the students should choose material that will be individually challenging at first. The students use these passages to practice reading with appropriate intonation, phrasing, and expression. Time is set aside each week for five to ten students to perform for classmates. Performances take no more than one minute each; usually they are much shorter than a minute.

Passages and poems that are used for performance reading can be cut apart at the phrase or sentence level and rebuilt by students working in centers or small groups. This strategy can be especially useful for English language learners, as it offers an additional opportunity to explore and internalize the structure of the English language.

Readers Theatre

Readers theatre is a dramatic experience that can be used to enhance students' engagement with literature as well as their reading fluency. Readers theatre is typically implemented with small groups.

1. Either choose a script or work with students to write a short script of their own. If students write their own, you or an adult volunteer can take dictation to facilitate the process. To differentiate, vary the difficulty of the parts. Be sure that English language learners understand the meaning of the script and adjust their parts as necessary to match their current facility with the language. English language learners may benefit from the addition of props and gestures for additional support (Rea and Mercuri 2006).

2. The script is read by students over and over for fluency (intonation, phrasing, and expression) rather than memorization. The script is practiced for a performance.

3. The script is performed for the class.

Documentary Clip Reading

Documentary clip reading is a whole-class activity that involves students in purposeful practice reading of individual texts. The end result is a class performance.

1. Select a theme for a documentary—for example, woodland animals, insects, sports figures, human relationships, diversity, a U.S. state, a key historical figure, or current events.

2. Using short familiar texts, students practice parts in class and are assigned to practice at home. Instruction is differentiated by varying

the difficulty of parts or by having students write their own parts. You may also work with some students in small groups to help them prepare.

3. For the presentations, the classroom is set up like a studio, with special chairs and lights for the readers.

Fluency Development Lesson (Rasinski et al. 1994)

The *fluency development lesson* is recommended for small groups and can be nested into the work of guided reading/intervention groups, if desired.

1. Read a short text as students silently follow along on their own selections.

2. Discuss the selection and your expressiveness during reading.

3. Chorally read the text several times.

4. Have students move into prearranged pairs and take turns reading the selection with expression.

5. Arrange for individuals to perform for some audience (even the small group will work).

6. Choose (with students) some critical words from the passage and use them for word study.

7. Send home a copy of the text for practice with family members.

8. Reread the passage from the previous day and work with the words again as appropriate.

9. The lesson routine begins again with step one.

Language Transcription

Language transcription involves students in talking about an experience, observing as an adult takes dictation, and then reading and rereading what has been written. It may be implemented with a small or large group or with individuals. If implementing the strategy within regular classroom instruction, the written product can be used for instruction within small groups. This strategy is especially valuable for developing word knowledge and building fluency, and it is widely recommended for use with English language learners.

1. Provide a prompt that leads the student(s) to talk about a familiar experience. Try to hone in on a personal/group narrative or a descriptive piece. Depending on your purposes, the piece may range from one to eight sentences. The following prompts may be useful:

   Let's write about . . .

   - something you have done at school so far
   - something you have seen at school so far
   - something special that has happened
   - something you do often
   - something you did when you were little
   - something you like to do
   - something you don't like to do
   - a special place
   - a special person
   - a special thing
   - something you like to play
   - something you know a lot about
   - how to do something
   - how to make something
   - something you have just learned about
   - something you have observed

2. After discussing the experience, indicate that you will now write the experience as it is dictated to you. Encourage a logical beginning, middle, and ending, using student language, but helping with revision of language if the written result will be unclear. As you write:

   - Emphasize how to stretch words to listen for their sounds.
   - Show students how to find words on the word wall and in other locations around the classroom.
   - Emphasize your choice of syntax and punctuation.

3. Provide a neat copy to each participating student. Have the student(s) read what was written.

For Students Needing Support Using Prereading Strategies

Three-Finger Rule (Allington 2006)

The *three-finger rule* lesson is implemented with the whole class to show students how to determine whether a book may require an extra effort to work through or be too challenging to learn from and enjoy. To implement the strategy, show students how to read the first one or two pages of a book (depending on the number of words) and raise a finger each time they cannot read a word. For beginning readers, three fingers represent a book that is probably too hard. It is generally recommended that books being read for independent reading can be read with an accuracy of above 95 percent. However, always keep in mind that interest and motivation can do a lot to facilitate comprehension. We don't want to keep kids from books they want to read just because they are not perfectly leveled for them.

Previewing

Previewing involves turning through the pages of the text to activate prior knowledge and take note of the content and structure. Students should be observed and supported as they preview within various genres to determine whether they are using this important comprehension strategy. The following procedures can be used to support student previewing and should be implemented with both fiction and nonfiction. The lesson can be implemented with small groups or the whole class and can be nested into the work of guided reading/intervention groups.

1. Choose a book for modeling, and have available a bin of books for partners to use. You may wish to have all students use either fiction or nonfiction the first few times you teach the previewing lesson. You can differentiate by having books representing a range of difficulty.

2. Show students the cover and tell them everything you notice (title, author, illustration, possible prediction). Show how you look to see if the back cover has any interesting information. Turn through the pages and show/describe any special features such as headers, captions, fonts, tables of contents, maps, graphs, or charts.

3. Discuss with students how a reader's purpose and goals affect the preview. For example, if you are reading nonfiction, there may be a specific part of the text you would read rather than the entire book. Show students how you would locate certain parts of the text depending on your purpose or goal.

4. Ask the students to turn through their books and note any special features.

5. Have students report their observations back to the class.

For Students Needing Support Engaging with Text

Guided Reading

Just as guided reading can be useful for supporting children's development of text processing strategies, it can be useful for supporting their development of comprehension and engagement strategies. When students are regularly guided through processes such as previewing, synthesizing, questioning, evaluating, and considering critical vocabulary, they develop *strategies* that support their comprehension as well as *dispositions* for engaging with text. Pages 233 and 234 provide generic lesson plans for guided reading with a focus on comprehension and engagement with meaning.

RTI Lesson Plan for Small Groups: Focus on Text Comprehending

Students: _____

Teacher: _____ Date: _____ Time: _____

Lesson Plan for Small Groups: Focus on Comprehending	Observations to Inform Next Lesson
Book: _____ Level _____	

1. **Previewing and Synthesizing**
   If the book is new: Students preview the book or section.

   If the book is in progress: Students work together to synthesize the part just read. Then, they discuss the content, with one student starting the conversation by providing an evaluation, question, or other response. Any challenging vocabulary is identified.

2. **Language Study**
   Students engage in language study using challenging or critical words or phrases they and teacher have identified. Graphic organizers may be used. Focus words or phrases:

   _____

3. **Teacher Modeling**
   Teacher uses part of the text to model and discuss the use of comprehension strategies. Comprehension strategies may include: previewing, identifying text structure, evaluating, questioning, inferring, summarizing, monitoring, and visualizing.

4. **Reading**
   Students continue reading silently where the teacher left off. Students may be pulled aside for miscue documentation or further work with strategies. A stopping point and plan for discussion are set for the next meeting.

5. **Response**
   Students prepare for the next day's discussion (step 1) by recording questions and/or observations.

RTI Lesson Plan for Small Groups: Focus on Text Comprehending with English Language Learners

Students: _____

Teacher: _____ Date: _____ Time: _____

Lesson Plan for Small Groups: Focus on Comprehending	Observations to Inform Next Lesson
Book: _____ Level _____ 1. **Previewing and Synthesizing** *If the book is new*: Students preview the book or section. *If the book is in progress*: Students work together to synthesize the part just read. Then, they discuss the content, with one student starting the conversation by providing an evaluation, question, or other response. Any challenging vocabulary and syntax or text structures are identified. 2. **Language Study** Students engage in language study using challenging or critical words, phrases, syntax, and structures they and teacher have identified. Graphic organizers are used as appropriate. Focus: _____ 3. **Teacher Modeling** Teacher uses part of the text to model and discuss the use of comprehension strategies. Comprehension strategies may include: previewing, identifying text structure, evaluating, questioning, inferring, summarizing, monitoring, and visualizing. Attention is paid to modeling how to solve complex aspects of syntax and meaning. 4. **Reading** Students continue reading silently or aloud where the teacher left off. Arrangements are made to check for understanding during the reading as appropriate. Students may be pulled aside for miscue documentation or further work with strategies. A stopping point and plan for discussion are set for the next meeting. 5. **Response** Students prepare for the next day's discussion (step 1) by recording questions and/or observations.	

Mindful Predicting

Readers are always predicting—using meaning and structure cues in the text along with background knowledge—to think about what might come next. For students who do not effectively tune into the developing meaning as they read, mindful predicting can be a useful strategy. This lesson can be implemented during class read-alouds or with small needs-based groups, and can be nested into guided reading lessons.

1. Select a piece of literature with good predictive quality. Almost any literature can be used, but the more knowledge your students have about the content and genre, the more in-depth their predictions will be. Therefore, consider whether the content will be familiar and also engaging for students to predict. With fiction, mysteries, races, challenges, character conflicts, and other life tensions can inspire lively conversations and can help students dig deeply into the strategy. With nonfiction, predictable events such as processes or life cycles can help to make the strategy obvious. Figure 2–1 provides a recommended short list for teaching and modeling the concept of predicting.

2. Model and explain the strategy of predicting with part of the text. Start by modeling a preview and then stating your predictions based on the title, illustrations, and any available text features. Read a part of the text and share a few further predictions.

3. After you model with part of the text, let students know that you will be stopping at certain points and asking them to share their predictions.

4. As you read, invite students to pair up to share their predictions.

Key Questions for Predicting

- What do you predict will happen/happen next? What from the book led you to make that prediction?

- What do you predict you will learn next?

- Are your predictions confirmed?

- How does predicting help you as a reader?

Figure 2–1 *Short List for Working with Predictions*

Level	Title and Author
B	*The Things Birds Eat*, by Betsey Chessen
D	*Too Many Balloons*, by Catherine Matthias
D	*From Egg to Robin*, by Suzan Canizares and Betsey Chessen
G	*Butterflies*, by Emily Neye
G	*It's a Good Thing There Are Insects*, by Allan Fowler
H	*Daniel's Mystery Egg*, by Alma Flor Ada
H	*A Tale of a Tadpole*, by Karen Wallace
I	*Ibis: A True Whale Story*, by John Himmelman
J	*Gus and Grandpa and the Two-Wheeled Bike*, by Claudia Mills
J	*From Seed to Plant*, by Allan Fowler
K	*Charlie Anderson*, by Barbara Abercrombie
K	*Koala Lou*, by Mem Fox
K	*A Log's Life*, by Wendy Pfeffer
M	*Too Many Tamales*, by Gary Soto
M	*From Seed to Plant*, by Gail Gibbons
O–P	*Two Bad Ants*, by Chris Van Allsburg

5. For students who need ongoing support, continue the prediction lessons in guided reading/intervention groups and encourage the habit of predicting during their independent reading. Some students may benefit (particularly when it comes to staying focused) from writing out a prediction before reading and coming back afterward to confirm or disconfirm it.

Mindful Questioning

Questioning is a natural and important part of meaning making, and all students can benefit from discussing the questions they generate while reading. Discussing questions sheds new light on content and also helps students understand the role of thinking in reading. Students who do not regularly engage with literature, or who do not engage deeply, can benefit from working with questioning as an engagement and comprehension strategy. The mindful questioning lesson can be implemented over time during class read-alouds or with small needs-based groups and can be embedded into guided reading work.

1. Select a rich piece of literature. In preparing for lessons focused on questioning, look for literature that will inspire your students' curiosity and wonderings or that they will find puzzling or challenging. Figure 2–2 features a recommended short list for teaching questioning with fiction. For teaching with nonfiction, select literature that is connected to the content areas your students are exploring.

2. Remind students that questions are a natural and important part of reading and can help readers engage with text and understand it in new ways. In fact, questioning might even send our reading in new directions or give it new energy.

3. Read aloud the book you have selected, and model the questions you have. Encourage the students to share their questions. Jot all questions on a piece of chart paper or on sticky notes that you can place in the book. As you continue reading and some of the questions are answered, check them off.

4. After reading, look back at the questions and discuss where the answers were found/could be found (in the text, in our schema, or through inferring). Reemphasize the important role that questioning—and discussing questions—can play for readers.

5. For students who need continued support to engage with text, continue the questioning lessons in guided reading/intervention groups, and encourage the habit of questioning during their independent reading.

2. Preview the text with the students. Let them know that upon completion of the reading, they will be asking you questions about the segment, and then you will ask them some questions.

3. Ask the students to read the first defined short segment, jotting down questions that come to mind. (You may read aloud to students who are not reading independently.)

4. Allow students to ask and discuss their questions. After the students ask their questions, you ask your questions. Continue this process with the other defined segments. Throughout the process, model and encourage effective questions that require deep thinking, integration of ideas across text, and using background knowledge.

5. Follow up with small groups and intervention groups as it is useful. Reciprocal questioning is an ideal strategy for both the classroom teacher and the intervention teacher to use, and it can be used in small groups to support content area reading.

Mindful Monitoring

Monitoring is a strategy that involves keeping track of meaning in a way that meets the purpose at hand and using repair strategies (rereading, rethinking, questioning, using illustrations, using text features, thinking aloud, discussing) when the reading becomes confusing or difficult. Especially when facing challenging text, students can benefit from *mindful monitoring*, which reminds them to think through and be sure they have grasped the meaning of text segment by segment. Mindful monitoring lessons can be implemented with the whole class or small groups and can be embedded into guided reading lessons.

1. Select a text to use for modeling. Look for literature that will challenge your students in terms of syntax, content, and/or structure. A rich story line that incorporates some challenging concepts or language or any text with tricky-to-navigate text features will work. What is considered challenging or tricky will depend on your students' experience with both oral and written language. Keep in mind that English language learners may need special instruction—beyond what your other students require—that sheds light on how to interpret complicated syntax, meanings, and structures. Figure 2–3 features a short list of texts that work well for modeling monitoring. The list contains

Figure 2–3 *Text Set for Working with Monitoring*

Level	Title and Author
L	*Sitti's Secrets*, by Naomi Shihab Nye
M	*Aunt Flossie's Hats (and Crab Cakes Later)*, by Elizabeth Fitzgerald Howe
M	*The Old Woman Who Named Things*, by Cynthia Rylant
M	*Miss Rumphius*, by Barbara Cooney
M	*Follow the Drinking Gourd*, by Jeanette Winter
M	*Coming On Home Soon*, Jacqueline Woodson
N	*The Lotus Seed*, by Sherry Garland
N	*Chicken Sunday*, by Patricia Polacco
N	*The Secret Footprints*, by Julia Alvarez
O–P	*So Far from the Sea*, by Eve Bunting
O–P	*Sequoyah*, by James Rumford
O–P	*A River Ran Wild*, by Lynne Cherry
O–P	*Mrs. Katz and Tush*, by Patricia Polacco
Q–R	*Train to Somewhere*, by Eve Bunting
U–W	*Shutting Out the Sky*, by Deborah Hopkinson
U–W	*Immigrant Kids*, by Russell Freedman

mostly fiction, as nonfiction texts are ideally selected within the content areas you are studying with your students.

2. Read the text aloud, modeling how to stop every so often to think through what you have read. Show students how to work through complexities and questions and use repair strategies when the text becomes tricky or confusing.

3. Team students up to read a passage or text together and discuss their monitoring activity.

4. Regularly follow up with small groups/intervention groups. Monitoring is a comprehension strategy that should be focused on daily.

- What have you wondered about? What has been confusing?

- What do you think the character *should* do at this point? What do you think the character *will* do? What would you do?

Nonfiction

- What has been interesting so far?

- What have you wondered about? What has been confusing?

- What has the author taught us so far?

- What is the author's point of view? Do you agree?

- Where do you think the author will take this next?

3. Bring the whole class back together to discuss their thinking about the book as well as any procedural aspects of the literature circles that need addressing.

For Students Needing Support
Identifying Main/Key Ideas

Retelling Guides

Many students do not know what is expected of them in a retelling or summary, and many have a difficult time pulling together the gist of what they have read and thinking it through in a logical sequence. Yet many comprehension standards/guidelines include the expectation that children will be able to produce a logically sequenced retelling.

Retelling guides are tools designed to help students carefully attend to text structure to rethink and revisit what they have read. They also serve as a useful tool for bringing key ideas to a "talking place" where they can be laid out and explored with others. The retelling guides on pages 246 and 247 each offer suggestions for what to include in a retelling (one for fiction and one for nonfiction). These may be used as wall charts, laminated teaching tools, or provided as individual handouts. Retelling guides may be embedded into group lessons/intervention sessions and used continually by classroom teachers and intervention teachers.

1. Select two pieces of literature (either fiction or nonfiction).

2. Begin the lesson by setting the purpose. Tell students that after they read or listen to a text, it's important that they are able to retell the key ideas. Thinking about key ideas as they read will help students focus as they read, and remember what is important. Tell students that you will use one of the books to model how you look for key ideas, and then you will have them try out the strategy on their own, using the other book.

3. Show students a guide that illustrates what you will retell/your expectations for their retellings. See pages 246 and 247 for examples to use in your classroom.

4. Model how you read and think about key ideas, referring to the guide as you go.

5. Tell students they will now be working through their own retelling and that you would like them to use the guide. Either read the student text aloud or allow time for students to read it independently or in groups. (To differentiate, you may read the text aloud to students who cannot do so independently and require that others read it independently.)

6. Support students as they work through the components of the guide.

Story Maps

Story maps (see pages 249–253) are a useful tool for rethinking text. They help the reader organize the content into a set of manageable elements. To complete a story map, students either write about or draw the elements on a map. When modeling how to use a story map, show students how to focus on writing just enough to spark a reminder of what happened. We do want students to include details as they rethink a text, but they do not need to spend excessive time writing them on a story map. For younger students, who may rely on drawing more than writing, do encourage detail in the drawing. The talk and thinking that occur during map creation, especially when students are given time to think through and share ideas, can serve as very useful ways to reflect on the material that has been read.

An alternative to story maps involves helping students think aloud as they "rebuild" the story using sticky notes. Students can place the notes in an arc to represent the rising and falling action. As an ultimate goal, we want students to focus on "construction of meaning" rather than leading them into an artificial "deconstruction of the text."

Story maps and sticky note retellings may be continually nested into small-group sessions as they are useful for helping students to construct meaning.

Story Sequencing Map

Name: _____ Date: _____

Title

Beginning

Middle

End

Name: JuLio   **Date:** 11-21

Story Sequencing Map

Title
Shotcut

Beginning
WeAReGOWING ONashotGut

Middle
UO aChRAN

End
Home

General Story Map

Name: _____ Date: _____

Title

Important Characters

Setting

Problem or Goal

Solution

Name: Bashira   **Date:** 12-5

General Story Map

Title: The BiggestSNOwballFight!

Characters	Setting
NO	

Problem or Goal	Resolution
?	

Detailed Story Map

Name: _____   Date: _____

Title

Characters

Setting

Key Events

Resolution or Ending

Informational Text Maps

Informational text maps are designed to help students focus on key ideas as they read and to help them organize their thinking about information gleaned from nonfiction. The informational text maps featured on pages 256 to 265 are specifically designed to support students in identifying and summarizing key ideas. These tools may be embedded into small-group sessions as they are useful to supporting students' knowledge building and construction of meaning.

- **Information web** (page 256): The information web is designed to help students categorically organize information that they want to remember from one or more texts. Webs are useful when students are working with text written in a descriptive format. The key idea or topic is written in the middle of the web, and specific categories for note taking are written in the blank spaces of the spokes. For example, the Lewis and Clark expedition might be a topic written in the middle of the web, with the notes being taken under the following categories: reasons for expedition, hardships, successes, Jefferson's role, Lewis and Clark's role, Sacagawea's role.

- **Cause and effect map** (page 257): The cause and effect map is designed to support students in thinking through the impacts that events or phenomena have on other events/phenomena.

- **Timeline** (page 258): Timelines are useful when students need to think through information in a sequence. Students write the topic in the top box, and in the boxes below, they write dates (or sequential numbers) with key information.

- **Comparison chart** (page 259): Comparison charts are designed to support students in recording key ideas or concepts about two related topics or phenomena, and then evaluating their similarities and differences. When using comparison charts, be sure that the comparisons support in-depth thinking. The activity should challenge children and require the use of text to learn and reflect on new concepts rather than serving as a tool to record what they know already or as an act of comparing just for the sake of comparing.

- **Cycle map** (pages 260 and 261): Cycle maps offer useful ways to depict and think through continuing or cyclical relationships such as the life cycle of an insect or the causes and effects of child labor. Page 260 provides a cycle map for writing and page 261 provides a cycle map for drawing.

- **Problem and solution chart** (page 262): Problem and solution charts work well with text that describes a particular problem or issue and presents a variety of hypothetical or real solutions. The charts help students to identify and consider key issues and compare the value of the varying solutions.

- **Ideas and details chart** (page 263): Ideas and details charts are a useful tool for helping students focus in on key information and the important details that support or surround that information.

Information Web

Name: _____ Date: _____

Cause and Effect Map

Name: _____ Date: _____

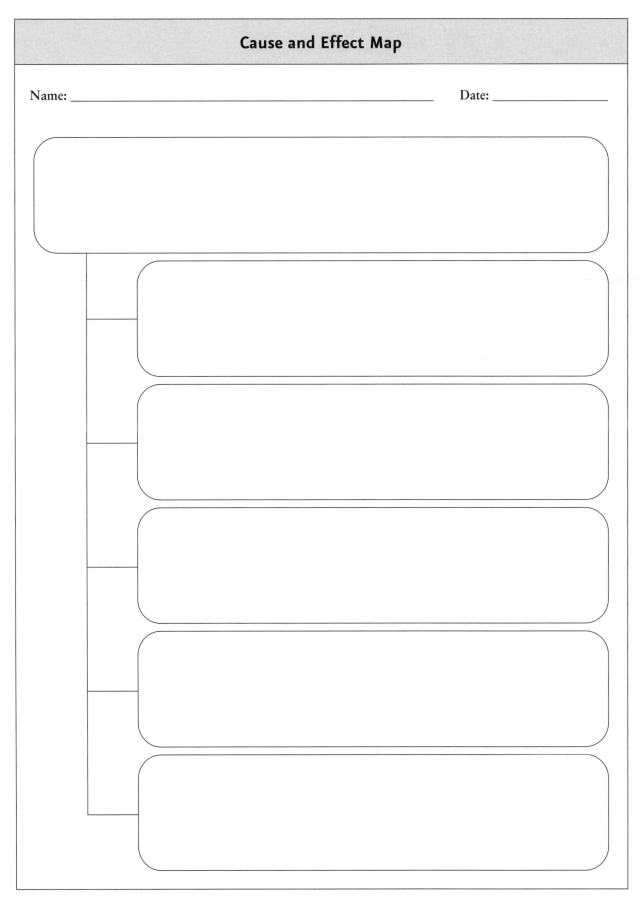

Timeline

Name: _____ Date: _____

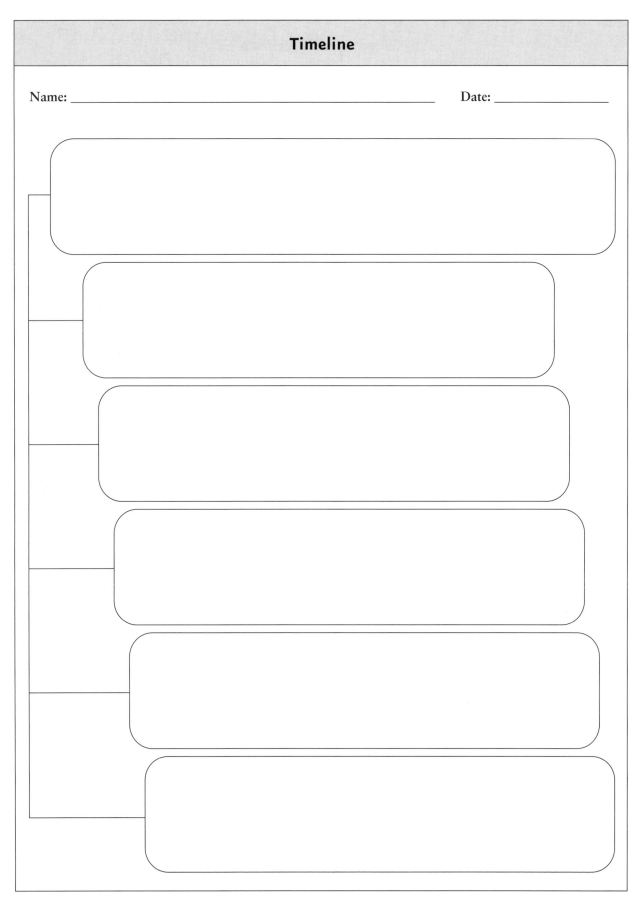

Comparison Chart

Name: _____ Date: _____

What I am comparing:

1.	2.

Cycle Map for Writing Information

Name: _____   Date: _____

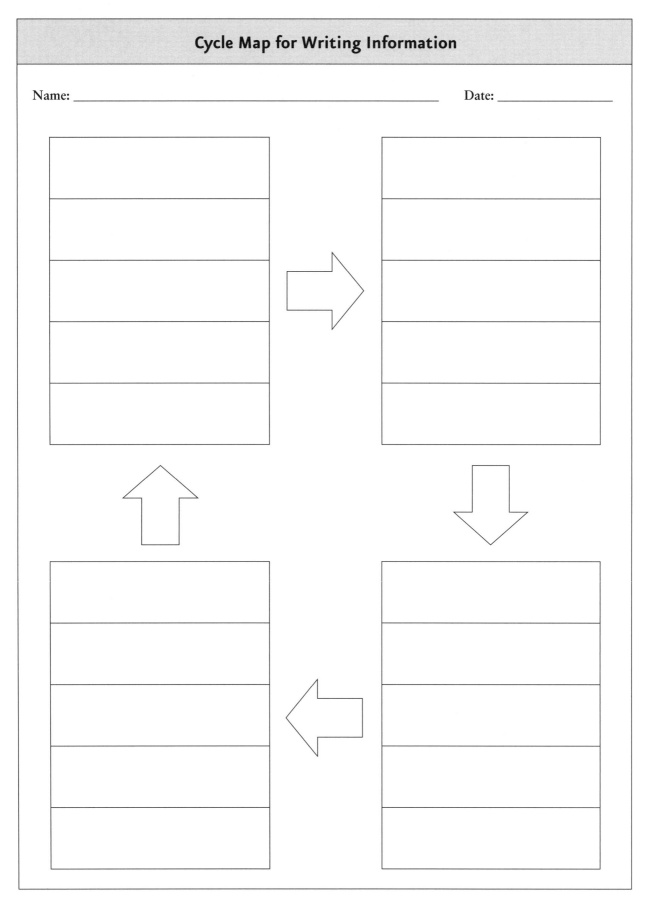

Name: _____   Date: _____

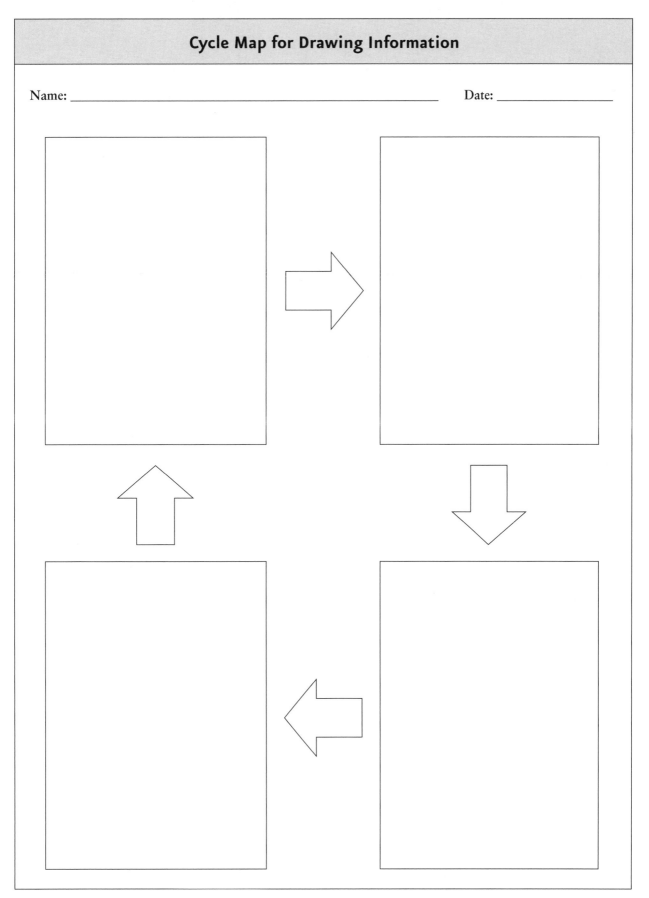

Problem and Solution Chart

Name: _____ Date: _____

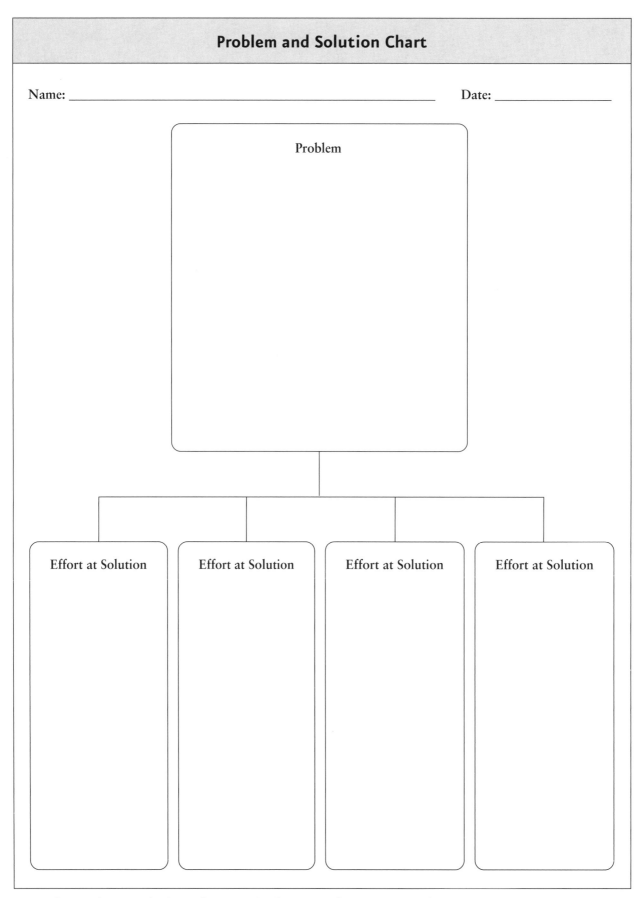

Problem

Effort at Solution

Effort at Solution

Effort at Solution

Effort at Solution

Ideas and Details Chart

Name: _____   Date: _____

Topic: _____

Book: _____

Important Ideas	Interesting Details

Name: **Michael 1st chapter** Date: _____

Ideas and Details Chart

Topic: The Discovery of a man 5000 years old

Book: Ice Mummy

Important Ideas	Interesting Details
• The man's skin • The clothes he was wearing • the snow level was down that year • the wood scattered around the man • Reinhold Messner thiks the wood is parts of toods,	• The mystery of the man's age • The carelessness of the police • the way the man is facing • that the police suggests the mummy was a hiker • How little effort the people put into escavating the man

Name: Alarie _____ Date: _____ __

Ideas and Details Chart

Topic: tigers _____

Book: The man-eating Tigers of Sundarbans _____

Important Ideas	Interesting Details
They ushaly don't kill humens Their good swimmers There are more tigers there then anywere elase in the world.	There are pink dolphans There are dangnus thing in the water Their great athlets

Retelling Centers

Retelling centers are used to support children in rethinking and discussing literature and are an ideal opportunity for children to learn from one another in a structured setting. English language learners especially can benefit from the opportunity that retelling offers for integrating oral language with meaningful reading and writing. A retelling center can be kept all year. The Retelling Center sidebar offers a set of activities that may be used with fiction and nonfiction text. To differentiate retelling experiences, for some of the activities you may wish to have bags of differently leveled texts with different students' names on the bags. For example, a kindergarten teacher might have a bag for books at the A–C level, the D and E level, and F–G.

Retelling Center

- Work with a partner. Look through the book and talk about the illustrations.

- Work with a partner. Read the book together, pausing to discuss and retell what you have read after every few pages.

- Make a set of puppets to retell the text.

- Draw a retelling. Include the characters, setting, problem, and solution.

- Use the sticky notes to mark key ideas as you read. Tell a friend about the key ideas.

- Retell into the tape recorder. Listen to your retelling.

- Create a web or map to retell.

Mindful Inferring

Inferring is a strategy that involves drawing conclusions about vocabulary and content using textual information as well as prior knowledge. For example, to deeply comprehend *Rose Blanche*, a Holocaust story (generally used with grades 5 and above) presented through the eyes of a young German girl, many levels of inferring are required: Why does the mayor wear a swastika? What do the yellow stars mean? Why was a boy being transported by soldiers? What is the significance of the camp being deserted at the end of the story? Though the author never tells us these things (inferring is all about filling in the gaps), thinking about their significance in a "mindful" way can enhance comprehension. As you teach inferring, keep in mind that what authors directly reveal *varies*, making some texts more difficult than others. Lessons related to inferring can be useful for all students, but particularly for those whose responses to text generally reflect lower-level thinking or little inferring and thinking beyond the text. Inferring lessons can be implemented with small groups or the whole class, and nested into guided reading lessons.

1. Select a piece of literature with complex content or vocabulary. When choosing, select pieces that your students may not quite "get" all the way or that require a deep level of inferring in order to fully appreciate the piece. Figure 2–4 provides a short list of recommended literature for teaching students about inferring.

2. Use the literature to model the process of inferring. Following are some key questions to guide the process:

   * What does this probably mean?

   * Why did the author or illustrator include this?

   * What does the author assume we know here?

   * What does the author probably want us to consider?

Figure 2-4 *Text Set for Working with Inferring*

Level	Title and Author
F	*What Will Fat Cat Sit On?*, by Jan Thomas
G	*No, David!*, by David Shannon
I	*The Little Mouse*, by Don and Audrey Wood
I	*Emma Kate*, by Patricia Polacco
K	*Don't Need Friends*, by Carolyn Crimi
L	*Something Beautiful*, by Sharon Dennis Wyeth
M	*Frida*, by Jonah Winter
M	*Dear Mrs. Larue*, by Mark Teague
M	*Precious and the Boo Hag*, by Patricia McKissack
N	*Faithful Elephants*, by Yukio Tsuchiya
O–P	*The Hickory Chair*, by Lisa Rowe Fraustino
O–P	*The Table Where Rich People Sit*, by Byrd Baylor
O–P	*Cheyenne Again*, by Eve Bunting
Q–R	*The Bracelet*, by Yoshiko Uchida
S–T	*How Many Days to America*, by Eve Bunting
U–W	*Rose Blanche*, Roberto Innocenti

3. Remind students that inferences are an important part of reading. There are times when significant information is not explained by the author. Instead, readers must infer the meaning of unknown words, or use prior knowledge, or use text clues in order to deeply understand what they are reading.

4. Regularly follow up with small groups/intervention groups. Inferring is a comprehension strategy that should be focused on daily.

Question Solving

Many students—even those designated by their teachers as top readers—have been observed to be capable of answering lower-level but not higher-level questions (Applegate, Applegate, and Modla 2009). *Question solving* is a teacher-guided strategy designed to support students in learning to consider varied question types. It may be used with small, needs-based groups or with the whole class and can be embedded into the work of guided reading groups.

1. To prepare for *Question solving*, develop a set of questions for students to answer as they read. Anywhere from three to six questions should suffice. It is recommended that you monitor the set to ensure that the questions are based on three levels of comprehension: literal, inferential, and critical (McKenna and Robinson 2002):

   - *Literal*: Reader locates facts that are stated in the text. Examples: How many years has the candidate been in office already? How many kinds of dolphins live in the ocean?

   - *Inferential*: Reader uses explicit facts and prior knowledge to generate conclusions. Examples: Which candidate is likely to win the election? What could be the consequences of failing to protect endangered dolphins?

   - *Critical*: Reader provides a knowledgeable value judgment. Examples: Which candidate would make a better president? Are human jobs and conveniences more important than the lives of dolphins?

2. Read through the set of questions with the students.

3. Choose one of the questions and model the type of thinking and reading that is necessary for finding the answer.

4. Arrange for students to work in pairs to develop answers to any of the remaining questions.

5. Students discuss how they developed answers to the questions and how the text supported this process.

6. As needed, continue to provide extra support for select students in small groups/intervention groups.

Collaborative Reasoning (Chinn and Anderson 1998)

Collaborative reasoning is a teacher-guided strategy that is recommended for small-group sessions. It can be nested into guided reading lessons. It is designed to encourage deep and thoughtful reading, and it helps students respond in thoughtful ways to critical questions about books.

1. Select a text that lends itself to taking a position on an issue. Students read silently with the knowledge that they will be asked to respond to and discuss a higher-level question when they are finished reading.

2. Pose a critical question that leads students to taking a position on an issue related to the text. For example, *Bessie Coleman: Daring Stunt Pilot* (Robbins 2007) tells the story of a woman who became America's first African American woman pilot. Throughout her life, she pays a price for various decisions she makes. A critical question could be: *Did Bessie Coleman make the right decision when she got involved in stunt flying?*

3. Students respond to the question with an initial agreement or disagreement, or they may respond with "not sure."

4. Students provide supporting evidence for their initial positions using personal experience and information from the text. They may change their positions as they weigh reasons and evidence presented by peers. The teacher's role is to support the reasoning process and encourage students to lead the discussion.

For Students Needing Support Developing Content and Vocabulary Knowledge

Gathering Information

Gathering information lessons are designed to help students prepare for reading on a specific topic. The process helps children build knowledge about the topic, provides a framework for discussing information with peers, and is good preparation for reading material with challenging new vocabulary and content.

1. Put together a text set on a topic that relates closely to your social studies or science curriculum. For example, you might choose as many books as you can find on the topic of insects, forces, sounds, or community workers.

2. Develop a question that will lead students to search for key information on a topic. For example, "Which animals migrate?" "How are different types of snakes born?" Even the youngest students can gather information by looking at the illustrations in well-chosen books. For example, you might ask, "When you look through these books, what are the different things you see birds eating?"

3. Model how to read through the text and document information through drawing or writing. Use the form on page 272 to record the topic, the question, and your findings.

4. Arrange for your students to engage in the same processes you have just modeled as they work in centers, teams, or small groups and to then share their findings.

Gathering Information from Text

Name: _____ Date: _____

Topic: _____

Question: _____

Findings:

Gathering Information from Text

Topic: BirDS

Question: WhAt DO BIrDSeAt ?

Findings:

1. MOTh
2. WeSL
1. SUN FLOWR
2. GRit
1. BUGS
1. WRMS
2. BARees
3. LISRD
4. mowS

What Do You Know Web

What Do You Know Web lessons (page 275) are implemented with the whole class or small groups as a way to build knowledge on a topic. They can be particularly helpful when students are likely to struggle with the material they must read due to lack of familiarity with the content or vocabulary.

1. Place students in groups to generate and share ideas about a topic to be read about or studied as part of the content curriculum. Page 275 provides a template for recording the information. You may suggest the word or phrase to place in the middle of the web.

2. Each group creates a web and then shares one key idea with the class.

Name: _____ Date: _____

Question and Answer Generation

Question and answer generation is a teaching strategy that helps students build knowledge on a particular topic. It is a useful strategy to use with students before they are assigned to read content they are likely to find new or challenging. The strategy can be implemented regularly as part of your content area teaching either with small groups or the whole class. The procedures are as follows:

1. Each student chooses a book that is related to what is being studied in science or social studies. This provides an important opportunity to differentiate. Each student should have text that is accessible.

2. Students preview the book by looking at the text features (table of contents, headings, illustrations, and so on).

3. Students decide on something they want to know more about as a result of the preview and write it down.

4. Students read and collaborate with peers to find out more about the topic.

5. Students use a web to record new information (see page 275).

6. Students share what they have learned.

Preview, Overview, Review (Goodman, Watson, and Burke 2005)

Preview, overview, review is a small-group or whole-class experience designed to support students in browsing a topic before reading assigned material on that topic. Initial browsing and talking helps students to develop some initial language and confidence that will facilitate more extensive movement into the material. This is especially useful for English language learners.

1. Set up a browsing table with a variety of material related to the topic. Materials may include books, articles, websites, and hands-on manipulatives.

2. Provide scheduled times for students to examine the materials in small groups.

3. When students have had a chance to browse the material, place them in groups of two or three. Ask them to create lists that indicate what they know about the topic.

4. Guide the students to organize the lists into categories by coming up with headings and listing appropriate items beneath or by creating a web with spokes to indicate subtopics.

5. Hold a whole-class meeting in which students share their lists with the class. As the students share their lists, make a web that includes all of the contributions.

Charting Questions and Answers

Charting questions and answers, typically used with informational texts, is a strategy designed to help students develop vocabulary and content knowledge before reading key material. Use the following procedures with the whole class to model the use of a question and answer chart (see pages 278 and 279):

1. Gather a set of books related to the content your students will be pursuing.

2. Think aloud about the general topic and discuss it with your students. Record curiosities generated by the discussion on a question and answer chart.

3. Make the texts you have collected available to students for working in teams of two. Ask them to find information about at least one of the recorded curiosities and record information about it on their own question and answer charts. As students work, observe and provide support as needed.

Question and Answer Chart

Name: _____   Date: _____

Topic: _____

Curiosities	What I Found

Questions, Answers, and References

Name: _____ Date: _____

Topic: _____

Curiosities	What I Found	Where I Found It

Key Word Study

Key word studies are designed to support deep exploration of the concepts and vocabulary in content-area reading material. The studies are implemented with small groups or the whole class and can be especially useful for English language learners, who often need specialized support to develop academic language proficiency.

1. After reading or listening to a section of text, students browse back through the material and select a set number of words (four to eight, depending on the length and density of the material) that they believe to be most important to understanding the material so far.

2. The teacher acts as scribe, listing the words and noting their location in the text.

3. Students work in teams to describe the meaning of each word, using examples and language from the book. The teacher acts as scribe.

Vocabulary Studies

Vocabulary studies are designed for students to study words within the wider context in which they appear. Helping students understand vocabulary in context can be facilitative of their comprehension. When students struggle with comprehension, it is often the case that vocabulary is what is getting in the way. English language learners especially may not know as many words as their native English-speaking peers, may not have knowledge of multiple meanings of words, and may have conversational proficiency but not the kind of academic vocabulary that will allow them to comprehend content material. Their still-developing knowledge of English syntax can create a barrier as well. When syntax is different and unfamiliar, this can make it difficult to use it to unlock context clues.

To implement vocabulary studies, select words that are critical to understanding the key concepts in a text or unit and use the graphic organizers to guide students to explore them from a variety of angles. Students may select the words as well. Pages 281 to 287 offer tools for vocabulary study. Work through the tools with the whole class, or model their uses, before setting students off to work in partner-teams or small groups. Vocabulary study may be nested into the language study phase of guided reading lessons. (See pages 219–220 and 233–234.)

Activating Prior Knowledge for Vocabulary

Name: _____ Date: _____

Instructions

1. Write down what you know about the focus word.

2. Read the text and discuss the focus word. Record what you have learned.

Word: _____

1. What I Knew Before the Study	2. What I Have Learned

Name: Piper

Date:

Activating Prior Knowledge for Vocabulary

Instructions
1. Write down what you know about the focus word. 2. Read the text and discuss the focus word. Record what you have learned.

Word: extrasolar planets

1. What I Knew Before the Study	2. What I Have Learned
I know that the book will be about planets. They will probably be planets that are solar, like our sun. I know that our sun is a star in the galacksy.	Extrasolar planets are planets atached to other suns out in space. They are so small that it is almost impossible to see them. Aliens could be found on them if we visited them.

Making a Word Hypothesis

Name: _____ Date: _____

Instructions

1. Read the text and then write what you think the word means.

2. Discuss the word and then add to your definition.

Word: _____

I think the word means . . .

After the discussion, I also understand . . .

Name: __Haley__ _____ Date: _____

Making a Word Hypothesis

Instructions

1. Read the text and then write what you think the word means.

2. Discuss the word and then add to your definition.

Word: __differ__ _____

I think the word means...

Do unusual things.

After the discussion, I also understand...

That it is very simaler to diffrent

Considering New Uses of Vocabulary

Name: _____ Date: _____

Word: _____

Word in the sentence

Definition

Another way it could be used in a sentence

Words with Meaningful Parts

Name: _____ Date: _____

Word: _____

Word in the sentence

Word broken into parts

Meaning of the parts

Other words with any of the parts

What It Is and What It Isn't

Name: _____ Date: _____

Word: _____

Word in the sentence

What it is	What it isn't

Resources for New Words

An important part of monitoring comprehension involves knowing strategies for determining the meanings of unknown words. To implement the *resources for new words* lessons, post and model the ten key strategies listed below.

- Predict or infer the meaning.

- Reread or read on to see if the meaning becomes clear.

- Check the surrounding sentences for a definition.

- Look at the parts.

- Use the illustrations.

- Try the glossary.

- Determine if it is worth taking the search beyond the text.

- Try a dictionary or thesaurus.

- Search the Internet.

- Ask someone.

Thematic Read-Alouds

Thematic read-alouds are designed to support student development of vocabulary related to a particular topic.

1. Select two to four books on a topic of importance to your content area studies (balance fiction with nonfiction).

2. Ask students to generate a list of words associated with the topic. As you record the words, add your own suggestions, making selections you know will be important to the topic.

3. Read the books (or sections) aloud to the group. Pause at key points to discuss the words on the list.

4. After reading, students record key words that are new to them and jot down the meanings. These can be kept in a word bank for students to use throughout the study.

Morphological Analysis

Morphological analysis is an instructional technique designed to support students in looking for meaning-based units in unfamiliar words they encounter. At the elementary level, students (usually starting around grade 3) are taught to look for recognizable prefixes and suffixes and also to take note of root words. A list of common prefixes and suffixes recommended for elementary-level instruction appears below in the Prefixes and Suffixes for Elementary Instruction box.

It is recommended for this age group that prefixes are examined for meaning and suffixes are identified primarily for removal, so that the *root* can aid in determining meaning (White, Sowell, and Yanagihara 1989). Morphological analysis can be especially useful to English language learners, because it supports their development of academic vocabulary.

Prefixes and Suffixes for Elementary Instruction		
Prefix	Meaning	Example
un	not	unsolved
dis	not	dishonest
in	not	inefficient
im	not	improbable
ir	not	irresponsible
non	not	nonsense
re	again or back	rearrange
en, em	(forms verb)	enrage
over	too much	overdo
mis	wrong	misunderstand

Suffixes: s, es, ed, ing, ly, er, or, ion, tion, ation, ition, ible, able, al, ial, y, ness

Based on White, Sowell, and Yanagihara (1989)

1. Select a focus word from the text to be read. Then, explore morphemes in the following ways:

   - Provide a list of four to six words with the same prefix (*rerun, redo, repaint, rework,* and *reappear*). Discuss the meanings of the words, and work together to construct a definition of the prefix. Discuss how to use the strategy (of dividing words into syllables and looking for meaningful parts) to figure out the meaning of unknown words while reading.

   - Provide a list of four to six words with the same suffix (*painter, teacher, runner, singer, dancer*). Discuss the meanings of the words, and work together to construct a definition of the suffix. Discuss how to use the strategy of dividing words into syllables and looking for meaningful parts to figure out the meaning of unknown words while reading.

2. Follow up by reading the text and discussing the focus word and its meaning in context. Encourage students to use morphological analysis while reading.

Language Structure Challenges

Language structure challenges involve children in teams working to analyze text and its parts. They can be especially useful for English language learners, who benefit from the opportunity to discuss and solve issues of language structure and syntax in a small-group setting.

- *Put together and read cut-up sentences.* Prepare a set of cut-up sentences that will be challenging but achievable for the participating students to reassemble. Store each sentence in a separate envelope. To help keep the pieces organized, number the envelopes and put the same number on the back of each word that goes in that envelope. Students move around the words until they have made a sentence. To differentiate, color-code the envelopes so that you know which are easier and which are harder.

- *Put together and read cut-up paragraphs.* Prepare a set of cut-up paragraphs that will be challenging but achievable for the participating students to reassemble in order. Store the sentences in one envelope, challenging students to play with the order until they have made a meaningful paragraph. To differentiate, color-code the envelopes so that you know which paragraphs are easier and which are harder.

- *Solve the meaning of passages with complex syntax and structure.* Photocopy a set of passages with varying uses of punctuation and syntax. Challenge groups to read their piece together and sort out the meaning. When they understand the piece and have worked out the complexities, they should read it aloud with expression.

Studying English Language Syntax

Syntactic differences between native and new languages can present a special challenge for English language learners. To explore issues of syntax, involve students in studying differences between the two languages. The following language study lesson is implemented with small groups and can be embedded into the *language study* phase of guided reading lessons.

1. Students each write a sentence of their choosing in the first language. You may require that the sentence relate to a book or a content area topic.

2. Students translate the words into English using sticky notes or small pieces of paper.

3. Students rebuild the sentences so that the syntax is appropriate for English, adding and changing words, word order, and punctuation as necessary.

4. Students and the teacher discuss the differences in syntax among the two languages.

RTI and Scientific Teaching

Teaching can be an ardently scientific act, and this is clearly evident in RTI classrooms where teachers maintain control over the curriculum and agency for their own decision making. In the best of situations, RTI teachers engage in systematic documentation, data collection, and data analysis. Based on their findings, they select and develop instructional practices they think will work well. Then, they observe again, to evaluate the growth that is occurring and to revise their instruction accordingly.

This book has taken you through a broad range of assessment and instructional practices that are designed for scientific teaching. You have encountered tools for estimating students' reading levels; strategies for targeting their needs; forms for assessing their growth over time; charts for determining whether the growth is satisfactory; and guidelines for using data to shape your instruction. Such practices are something more than research-*based*; they are scientific in and of themselves. *You* are doing the science.

An exciting part of scientific teaching is that it makes sensible the possibility of teacher control over the curriculum. With *data* in hand—the kind that are collected as students engage in real acts of reading—we know what our students know and can do, and we can confidently take charge of their instruction. We don't need scripts or prescribed series of lessons because our knowledgeable observations have given us a detailed sense of how and what to teach. We can try out instructional practices that have a good reputation for working (this is the research-*based* part), including material from published programs, and because we have good assessment practices in place, we can determine whether those practices are working with *our* particular students. This is the part that brings the practice from research-*based* to research *itself*. If the practices aren't working, or aren't working for some students, we can adapt and adjust them—or even scrap them—as our intuition suggests.

Intuition is an important part of what makes scientific teaching work—but not just *anybody* can enact it. Einstein (2008) pointed out that an act of scientific intuition can only be achieved when we watch with the "necessary attention" and when we have sufficient understanding of the field in question. In reading instruction, intuition requires a dynamic transaction between observation of kids as they read and professional knowledge about how literacy develops.

My friend Melissa tells the story of a fifth-grade boy she once taught. Adam was knowledgeable and articulate, but struggled with reading. Both comprehension and decoding concerns were keeping him from reading what many other students in the class could read and understand with ease.

When it was time for literature circles to begin, Melissa provided the students with a range of book choices (of varying levels and varying content), asking them to write down their preferences in rank order. Her plan was to place the students in groups based on their rankings and allow them to read their topmost choice if possible. If necessary, she would go with the second or third choice as a way to ensure that the book would be suitable in terms of accessibility. Her goal was for all students to experience success and engagement, and she was well set up to make this happen. Adam's top five choices? See the box at the top of page 295 for his rank-oriented preferences.

Because Melissa had done careful assessments of Adam's reading and his background and personal characteristics, she was worried. She worried that the text would be too hard to decode without an overwhelming amount of support; that his comprehension would suffer; that his confidence would falter; and that his literature circle experience would be less than satisfactory. Students who struggle are often on the affective "edge": very close to falling into low self-confidence, low motivation, and little desire to read. Melissa had been working protectively to keep Adam safe from sliding off because she knew that the scramble back up would be hard. But she didn't want to discourage this unexpected interest in *Hatchet*, one that might mean a breakthrough in his progress. Because of his strong interest in the content, and an exercising of her own intuition about the role of interest in reading, Melissa took the risk and let him go with the book.

Adam, who had been disengaged and becoming quite frustrated, finished the novel before everyone else in his group—plus read the sequel. Then he announced to the whole class, "This sequel sucks."

1. *Hatchet*

2. *Hatchet*

3. *Hatchet*

4. *Hatchet*

5. *Hatchet*

Adam had independently read two books within the course of three weeks. He had an opinion about the books that could only have come from deeply comprehending the material. And he had enthusiasm for more reading.

As teachers we often face assessments that are required, instructional programs that are required, curricula that are required, and guidelines we must follow. This won't go away in the near future, but we *can* work productively within such contexts. We *can* "personalize" within the requirements. Good teaching like Melissa's has always emerged from teachers' "right there" observations; from their making of instructional decisions based on knowledge of their particular students; and from their exercising of intuition to meet each child's needs. As you work within an RTI framework, watch your kids thoughtfully. Be confident to go forth with your intuitions. Share your thinking with others. And keep developing your professional knowledge. Working thoughtfully within an RTI framework, and working to improve the practices within it, you will be making a difference in children's lives.

Recommended Literature
for Assessment and Instruction

Grade Level	Book Level	Title	Author	Genre
K	A	*Can I Have a Pet?*	Hooks, Gwendolyn Hudson	F PB
K	A	*Good Night, Gorilla*	Rathmann, Peggy	F PB
K	A	*We Play Music*	Johnson, Dolores	F PB
K	A	*I Can Read*	Williams, Rozanne	NF
K	A	*What Do Insects Do?*	Canizares, Susan, and Chanko, Pamela	NF
K	A	*On Our Farm*	Williams, Laura	NF
K–1	B	*My Big Rock*	Perry, Phyllis	F PB
K–1	B	*Big Snowball Fight*	Figueredo, D. H.	F PB
K–1	B	*Cold and Hot*	Sweeney, Jacqueline	F PB
K–1	B	*Bath Time*	Malka, Lucy	F PB
K–1	B	*Monkeys*	Canizares, Susan	NF
K–1	B	*The Things Birds Eat*	Chessen, Betsey	NF
K–1	C	*Where Is My Puppy?*	Hatton, Caroline	F PB
K–1	C	*Cleaning Day*	Figueredo, D. H.	F PB
K–1	C	*Laundry Day*	French, Vivian	F PB
K–1	C	*Time for Tacos*	Golembe, Carla	NF
K–1	C	*I Eat Leaves*	Vandine, JoAnn	NF
K–1	C	*Fish Print*	Cappelini, Mary	NF
1	D	*I Had a Hippopotamus*	Lee, Hector Viveros	F PB
1	D	*Big Dog and Little Dog*	Pilkey, Dav	F PB
1	D	*Too Many Balloons*	Matthias, Catherine	F PB
1	D	*Splat!*	Perez-Mercado, Mary Margaret	F PB

Grade Level	Book Level	Title	Author	Genre
1	D	*Make a Turkey*	Suen, Anastasia	NF
1	D	*Frogs*	Canizares, Susan, and Moreton, Daniel	NF
1	D	*From Egg to Robin*	Canizares, Susan, and Chessen, Betsey	NF
1	E	*The Dashiki*	Taylor, Gaylia	F PB
1	E	*Who Is Coming?*	McKissack, Patricia	F PB
1	E	*Seven Cookies*	Heydenburk, Lorena Iglesias	F PB
1	E	*Cori Plays Football*	Florie, Christie	F PB
1	E	*I Need to Ask You Something*	Marx, Miriam	F PB
1	E	*Detective Dog and the Search for Cat*	Hill, Sandi	F PB
1	E	*Bengal Tiger*	Eckart, Edana	NF
1	E	*Gray Wolf*	Eckart, Edana	NF
1	F	*Chinatown Adventure*	Williams, Laura	F PB
1	F	*Today I Will Fly!*	Willems, Mo	F PB
1	F	*Ruby's Whistle*	Londner, Renee	F PB
1	F	*Cookie's Week*	Ward, Cynthia	F PB
1	F	*Not a Box*	Portis, Antoinette	F PB
1	F	*There Is a Bird on Your Head!*	Willems, Mo	F PB
1	F	*What Will Fat Cat Sit On?*	Thomas, Jan	F PB
1	F	*Dolphins*	James, Sylvia	NF
1	F	*Manatees*	Rustad, Martha	NF
1	G	*Hondo and Fabian*	McCarty, Peter	F PB
1	G	*Alligator Shoes*	Dorros, Michael	F PB
1	G	*Five Silly Fishermen*	Edwards, Roberta	F PB
1	G	*Mouse Went Out to Get a Snack*	McFarland, Lyn Rossiter	F PB
1	G	*Tough Boris*	Fox, Mem	F PB
1	G	*No, David!*	Shannon, David	F PB
1	G	*Milk to Ice Cream*	Snyder, Inez	NF
1	G	*Butterflies*	Neye, Emily	NF
1	G	*Giant Pandas*	Freeman, Marcia	NF
1	G	*It's a Good Thing There Are Insects*	Fowler, Allan	NF
1–2	H	*A Little Story About a Big Turnip*	Zunshine, Tatiana	F PB
1–2	H	*The Biggest Snowball Fight!*	Medearis, Angela	F PB
1–2	H	*Crocodile and Hen*	Lexau, Joan	F PB
1–2	H	*George Shrinks*	William, Joyce	F PB

Grade Level	Book Level	Title	Author	Genre
1–2	H	*The Mystery of the Cheese*	Harrison, Paul, and Rivers, Ruth	F PB
1–2	H	*Daniel's Mystery Egg*	Ada, Alma Flor	F PB
1–2	H	*Hi! Fly Guy*	Arnold, Tedd	F CB
1–2	H	*Feeding Time*	Lee, Davis	NF
1–2	H	*What Boo and I Do*	Williams, Laura	NF
1–2	H	*Tale of a Tadpole*	Wallace, Karen	NF
1–2	I	*Emma Kate*	Polacco, Patricia	F PB
1–2	I	*Widget*	McFarland, Lyn Rossiter	F PB
1–2	I	*Hattie and the Fox*	Fox, Mem	F PB
1–2	I	*Surprise Moon*	Hatton, Caroline	F PB
1–2	I	*Froggy Goes to School*	London, Jonathan	F PB
1–2	I	*The Little Mouse*	Wood, Don and Audrey	F PB
1–2	I	*Tiny Life on Your Body*	Taylor-Butler, Christine	NF
1–2	I	*Red-Eyed Tree Frog*	Cowley, Joy	NF
1–2	I	*Two Eyes, a Nose, and a Mouth*	Intrater, Roberta Grobel	NF
1–2	I	*Truck Trouble*	Royston, Angela	NF
2	J	*Amazing Grace*	Hoffman, Mary	F PB
2	J	*Big Mama and Grandma Ghana*	Medearis, Angela Shelf	F PB
2	J	*Owl at Home*	Lobel, Arnold	F PB
2	J	*Henry and Mudge and the Great Grandpas*	Rylant, Cynthia	F CB
2	J	*The Mystery of the Missing Dog*	Levy, Elizabeth	F CB
2	J	*A Giraffe Calf Grows Up*	Hewett, Joan	NF
2	J	*A Koala Joey Grows Up*	Hewett, Joan	NF
2	J	*Fantastic Planet*	Kenah, Katharine	NF
2	J	*Dinosaur Dinners*	Davis, Lee	NF
2	K	*Charlie Anderson*	Abercrombie, Barbara	F PB
2	K	*Abuela*	Dorros, Arthur	F PB
2	K	*Koala Lou*	Fox, Mem	F PB
2	K	*The Good Luck Cat*	Harjo, Joy	F PB
2	K	*Amazing Grace*	Hoffman, Mary	F PB
2	K	*Don't Need Friends*	Crimi, Carolyn	F PB
2	K	*Mercy Watson Goes for a Ride*	DiCamillo, Kate	F CB
2	K	*Nate the Great*	Sharmat, Marjorie Weinman	F CB
2	K	*A Log's Life*	Pfeffer, Wendy	NF
2	K	*Martin's Big Words*	Rappaport, Doreen	NF
2	K	*Cheetahs*	St. Pierre, Stephanie	NF
2	K	*Ibis: A True Whale Story*	Himmelman, John	NF
2	K	*Monarch Butterfly*	Gibbons, Gail	NF

Grade Level	Book Level	Title	Author	Genre
2–3	L	*The Lost Lake*	Say, Allen	F PB
2–3	L	*My Buddy*	Osofsky, Audrey	F PB
2–3	L	*Sitti's Secrets*	Nye, Naomi Shihab	F PB
2–3	L	*Something Beautiful*	Wyeth, Sharon Dennis	F PB
2–3	L	*Cowgirl Kate and Cocoa*	Lewin, Betsy	F CB
2–3	L	*The Case of the Cool-Itch Kid*	Giff, Patricia Reilly	F CB
2–3	L	*Cam Jansen: The Mystery of the Missing Dinosaur Bones*	Adler, David	F CB
2–3	L	*Judy Moody Was in a Mood*	McDonald, Megan	F CB
2–3	L	*Jaguars*	Squire, Ann	NF
2–3	L	*Just for Elephants*	Buckley, Carol	NF
2–3	L	*Leopards*	St. Pierre, Stephanie	NF
2–3	L	*Oil Spill!*	Berger, Melvin	NF
2–3	L	*How It Was with Dooms: A True Story from Africa*	Hopcraft, Xan and Carol	NF
2–3	M	*Too Many Tamales*	Soto, Gary	F PB
2–3	M	*The Other Side*	Woodson, Jacqueline	F PB
2–3	M	*Henry's Freedom Box*	Levine, Ellen	F PB
2–3	M	*Show Way*	Woodson, Jacqueline	F PB
2–3	M	*Aunt Flossie's Hats (and Crab Cakes Later)*	Howe, Elizabeth Fitzgerald	F PB
2–3	M	*The Old Woman Who Named Things*	Rylant, Cynthia	F PB
2–3	M	*Miss Rumphius*	Cooney, Barbara	F PB
2–3	M	*Follow the Drinking Gourd*	Winter, Jeanette	F PB
2–3	M	*Coming On Home Soon*	Woodson, Jacqueline	F PB
2–3	M	*Dear Mrs. LaRue*	Teague, Mark	F PB
2–3	M	*Precious and the Boo Hag*	McKissack, Patricia	F PB
2–3	M	*Solo Girl*	Pinkney, Andrea Davis	F CB
2–3	M	*Marvin Redpost: Kidnapped at Birth?*	Sachar, Louis	F CB
2–3	M	*The Story of Chocolate*	Polin, C. J.	NF
2–3	M	*From Seed to Plant*	Gibbons, Gail	NF
2–3	M	*A Horse Named Seabiscuit*	Dubowski, Mark	NF
2–3	M	*Koko's Kitten*	Patterson, Francine	NF
2–3	M	*Home to Medicine Mountain*	Santiago, Chiori	NF
2–3	M	*Frida*	Winter, Jonah	NF
3	N	*The Gold Coin*	Ada, Alma Flor	F PB
3	N	*Dolphin's First Day*	Zoehfeld, Kathleen	F PB
3	N	*Heroes*	Mochizuki, Ken	F PB

Grade Level	Book Level	Title	Author	Genre
3	N	*Zen Shorts*	Muth, Jon	F PB
3	N	*The Lotus Seed*	Garland, Sherry	F PB
3	N	*Chicken Sunday*	Polacco, Patricia	F PB
3	N	*The Secret Footprints*	Alvarez, Julia	F PB
3	N	*The Year of the Panda*	Schlein, Miriam	F CB
3	N	*Hannah*	Whelan, Gloria	F CB
3	N	*Catwings*	LeGuin, Ursula	F CB
3	N	*Coolies*	Soentpiet, Chris	F CB
3	N	*Titanic*	Sherrow, Victoria	NF
3	N	*Saving Samantha*	Van Frankenhuyzen, Robbyn	NF
3	N	*The Milk Makers*	Gibbons, Gail	NF
3	N	*Why Frogs Are Wet*	Hawes, Judy	NF
3	N	*Adopted by an Owl*	Van Frankenhuyzen, Robbyn	NF
3	N	*Dirt*	Tomecek, Steve	NF
3	N	*Faithful Elephants*	Yukio, Tsuchiyo	NF
3	N	*Journey: Stories of Migration*	Rylant, Cynthia	NF
3–4	O–P	*Cheyenne Again*	Bunting, Eve	F PB
3–4	O–P	*Two Bad Ants*	Van Allsburg, Chris	F PB
3–4	O–P	*Baseball Saved Us*	Mochizuki, Ken	F PB
3–4	O–P	*Henry's Freedom Box*	Levine, Ellen	F PB
3–4	O–P	*Show Way*	Woodson, Jacqueline	F PB
3–4	O–P	*The Ghost Dance*	McLerran, Alice	F PB
3–4	O–P	*So Far from the Sea*	Bunting, Eve	F PB
3–4	O–P	*Mrs. Katz and Tush*	Polacco, Patricia	F PB
3–4	O–P	*The Hickory Chair*	Fraustino, Lisa Rowe	F PB
3–4	O–P	*The Table Where Rich People Sit*	Baylor, Byrd	F PB
3–4	O–P	*Indian Shoes*	Smith, Cynthia Leitich	F CB
3–4	O–P	*Stone Fox*	Gardiner, John Reynolds	F CB
3–4	O–P	*Sideways Stories from Wayside School*	Sachar, Louis	F CB
3–4	O–P	*Mummies: Secrets of the Dead*	Raleigh, Richard	NF
3–4	O–P	*Ice Mummy*	Dubowski, Mark and Cathy	NF
3–4	O–P	*Horse Heroes* (short story collection)	Petty, Kate	NF
3–4	O–P	*Sequoyah*	Rumford, James	NF
3–4	O–P	*A River Ran Wild*	Cherry, Lynne	NF
4	Q–R	*Train to Somewhere*	Bunting, Eve	F PB
4	Q–R	*Because of Winn-Dixie*	DiCamillo, Kate	F CB

Grade Level	Book Level	Title	Author	Genre
4	Q–R	*Hatchet*	Paulsen, Gary	F CB
4	Q-R	*Every Living Thing* (short story collection)	Rylant, Cynthia	F CB
4	Q-R	*Diary of a Wimpy Kid*	Kinney, Jeff	F CB
4	Q-R	*The Girl-Son*	Neuberger, Anne	F CB
4	Q-R	*Original Adventures of Hank the Cowdog*	Erickson, John	F CB
4	Q-R	*The Bracelet*	Uchida, Yoshiko	F CB
4	Q-R	*The Great Kapok Tree*	Cherry, Lynne	F CB
4	Q-R	*The Story of Muhammad Ali*	Garrett, Leslie	NF
4	Q-R	*Harvesting Hope: The Story of Cesar Chavez*	Krull, Kathleen	NF
4	Q-R	*The Man-Eating Tigers of the Sundarbans*	Montgomery, Sy	NF
4	Q-R	*The Snake Scientist*	Montgomery, Sy	NF
4	Q-R	*All About Owls*	Arnosky, Jim	NF
4	Q-R	*All About Deer*	Arnosky, Jim	NF
4	Q-R	*Pirates! Raiders of the High Seas*	Maynard, Christopher	NF
4–5	S–T	*The Butterfly*	Polacco, Patricia	F PB
4–5	S–T	*How Many Days to America?*	Bunting, Eve	F PB
4–5	S–T	*Joey Pigza Swallowed the Key*	Gantos, Jack	F CB
4–5	S–T	*Altogether–One at a Time* (short story collection)	Konigsburg, E. L.	F CB
4–5	S–T	*The Birchbark House*	Erdrich, Louise	F CB
4–5	S–T	*Taking Sides*	Soto, Gary	F CB
4–5	S–T	*Buffalo Hunt*	Freedman, Russell	NF
4–5	S–T	*The Great Ships*	O'Brien, Patrick	NF
4–5	S–T	*Out of Darkness*	Freedman, Russell	NF
4–5	S–T	*Crazy Cars*	Doeden, Mat	NF
4–5	S–T	*Wolves*	Simon, Seymour	NF
5–6	U–W	*Rose Blanche*	Innocenti, Roberto	F PB
5–6	U–W	*Esperanza Rising*	Ryan, Pam Muñoz	F CB
5–6	U–W	*Wringer*	Spinelli, Jerry	F CB
5–6	U–W	*A Long Way from Chicago*	Peck, Richard	F CB
5–6	U–W	*The Watsons Go to Birmingham*	Curtis, Christopher Paul	F CB
5–6	U–W	*Around the World in a Hundred Years*	Fritz, Jean	NF
5–6	U–W	*A Boy Called Slow*	Bruchac, Joseph	NF
5–6	U–W	*Buried in Ice*	Beattie, Owen, and Geiger, John	NF

Grade Level	Book Level	Title	Author	Genre
5–6	U–W	*Faraway Worlds: Planets Beyond Our Solar System*	Halpern, Paul	NF
5–6	U–W	*Immigrant Kids*	Freedman, Russell	NF
5–6	U–W	*The Tarantula Scientist*	Montgomery, Sy	NF
6	X–Z	*Maximum Ride*	Patterson, James	F CB
6	X–Z	*Touching Spirit Bear*	Mikaelson, Ben	F CB
6	X–Z	*Gathering Blue*	Lowry, Lois	F CB
6	X–Z	*Owen and Mzee*	Hatkoff, Craig	NF
6	X–Z	*Shutting Out the Sky*	Hopkinson, Deborah	NF
6	X–Z	*Escapes!*	Scandiffio, Laura	NF
6	X–Z	*The Wildlife Detectives*	Jackson, Donna	NF
6	X–Z	*Oh, Rats!*	Marrin, Albert	NF
6	X–Z	*Indian Chiefs*	Freedman, Russell	NF
6	X–Z	*Cowboys of the Wild West*	Freedman, Russell	NF
6	X–Z	*Quest for the Tree Kangaroo*	Montgomery, Sy	NF

Tracking Forms for the Reading Assessments, K–6

Tracking Form for the Reading Assessment

Student _____ Teacher _____ Grade __K__

Initial Assessment Date: _____ Intervention Starting Date (draw line to indicate): _____

Chart the student's highest instructional level. For a level to be designated as highest instructional, the examiner must determine the "too-hard" point, and then move down a level. The student must have a comprehension score of at least 60% *and* an accuracy score of at least 90%.	X–Z																	
	U–W																	
	S–T																	
	Q–R																	
	O–P																	
	N																	
	M																	
	L																	
	K																	
	J																	
	I																	
	H																	
	G																	
	F																	
	E																	
	D																	
	C																	
	B																	
	A																	

	Text Levels	Sept		Oct		Nov		Dec		Jan		Feb		Mar		Apr		May
List texts and levels used for the assessment.																		

Tracking Form for the Reading Assessment

Student _____ Teacher _____ Grade __1__

Initial Assessment Date: _____ Intervention Starting Date (draw line to indicate): _____

Chart the student's highest instructional level. For a level to be designated as highest instructional, the examiner must determine the "too-hard" point, and then move down a level. The student must have a comprehension score of at least 60% *and* an accuracy score of at least 90%.

Level									
X–Z									
U–W									
S–T									
Q–R									
O–P									
N									
M									
L									
K									
J									
I									
H									
G									
F									
E									
D									
C									
B									
A									
Text Levels	Sept	Oct	Nov	Dec	Jan	Feb	Mar	Apr	May

List texts and levels used for the assessment.

Tracking Form for the Reading Assessment

Student _____ Teacher _____ Grade __2__

Initial Assessment Date: _____ Intervention Starting Date (draw line to indicate): _____

Chart the student's highest instructional level. For a level to be designated as highest instructional, the examiner must determine the "too-hard" point, and then move down a level. The student must have a comprehension score of at least 60% *and* an accuracy score of at least 90%.

Level		Sept		Oct		Nov		Dec		Jan		Feb		Mar		Apr		May	
X–Z																			
U–W																			
S–T																			
Q–R																			
O–P																			
N																			
M														▓	▓	▓	▓	▓	
L														▓	▓	▓	▓	▓	▓
K								▓	▓	▓	▓	▓							
J								▓	▓	▓	▓	▓							
I		▓	▓	▓	▓	▓													
H		▓	▓	▓	▓	▓													
G																			
F																			
E																			
D																			
C																			
B																			
A																			
Text Levels		Sept		Oct		Nov		Dec		Jan		Feb		Mar		Apr		May	

List texts and levels used for the assessment.

© 2010 by Gretchen Owocki, from *The RTI Daily Planning Book, K–6*. Portsmouth, NH: Heinemann.

Tracking Form for the Reading Assessment

Student _____ Teacher _____ Grade __3__

Initial Assessment Date: _____ Intervention Starting Date (draw line to indicate): _____

Chart the student's highest instructional level. For a level to be designated as highest instructional, the examiner must determine the "too-hard" point, and then move down a level. The student must have a comprehension score of at least 60% *and* an accuracy score of at least 90%.	X–Z																		
	U–W																		
	S–T																		
	Q–R																		
	O–P																		
	N																		
	M																		
	L																		
	K																		
	J																		
	I																		
	H																		
	G																		
	F																		
	E																		
	D																		
	C																		
	B																		
	A																		
	Text Levels	Sept		Oct		Nov		Dec		Jan		Feb		Mar		Apr		May
	List texts and levels used for the assessment.																	

Student _____ Teacher _____ Grade __4__

Initial Assessment Date: _____ Intervention Starting Date (draw line to indicate): _____

Chart the student's highest instructional level. For a level to be designated as highest instructional, the examiner must determine the "too-hard" point, and then move down a level. The student must have a comprehension score of at least 60% *and* an accuracy score of at least 90%.

Level																		
X–Z																	
U–W																	
S–T												▓	▓	▓	▓	▓	▓
Q–R						▓	▓	▓	▓	▓							
O–P	▓	▓	▓	▓	▓												
N																	
M																	
L																	
K																	
J																	
I																	
H																	
G																	
F																	
E																	
D																	
C																	
B																	
A																	
Text Levels	Sept		Oct		Nov		Dec		Jan		Feb		Mar		Apr		May

List texts and levels used for the assessment.

Tracking Form for the Reading Assessment

Student _____ Teacher _____ Grade __5__

Initial Assessment Date: _____ Intervention Starting Date (draw line to indicate): _____

Chart the student's highest instructional level. For a level to be designated as highest instructional, the examiner must determine the "too-hard" point, and then move down a level. The student must have a comprehension score of at least 60% *and* an accuracy score of at least 90%.

		Sept	Oct	Nov	Dec	Jan	Feb	Mar	Apr	May
X–Z										
U–W										
S–T										
Q–R										
O–P										
N										
M										
L										
K										
J										
I										
H										
G										
F										
E										
D										
C										
B										
A										
Text Levels		Sept	Oct	Nov	Dec	Jan	Feb	Mar	Apr	May

List texts and levels used for the assessment.

Tracking Form for the Reading Assessment

Student _____ Teacher _____ Grade __6__

Initial Assessment Date: _____ Intervention Starting Date (draw line to indicate): _____

Chart the student's highest instructional level. For a level to be designated as highest instructional, the examiner must determine the "too-hard" point, and then move down a level. The student must have a comprehension score of at least 60% *and* an accuracy score of at least 90%.	X–Z																	
	U–W																	
	S–T																	
	Q–R																	
	O–P																	
	N																	
	M																	
	L																	
	K																	
	J																	
	I																	
	H																	
	G																	
	F																	
	E																	
	D																	
	C																	
	B																	
	A																	
	Text Levels	Sept		Oct		Nov		Dec		Jan		Feb		Mar		Apr		May
	List texts and levels used for the assessment.																	

Allington, R. 2001. *What Really Matters for Struggling Readers: Designing Research-Based Programs.* New York: Addison-Wesley.

———. 2002. "What I've Learned About Effective Reading Instruction from a Decade of Studying Exemplary Elementary Classroom Teachers." *Phi Delta Kappan* 83 (10): 740–47.

———. 2006. *What Really Matters for Struggling Readers: Designing Research-Based Programs.* 2d ed. New York: Longman.

———. 2007. "Allington on RTI: An IRA Insights Podcast." Available at http://146.145.202.164/downloads/podcasts/II-Allington.mp3.

———. 2009. *What Really Matters in Response to Intervention: Research-Based Designs.* Boston: Allyn and Bacon.

Applegate, M., A. Applegate, and V. Modla. 2009. "'She's My Best Reader; She Just Can't Comprehend': Studying the Relationship Between Fluency and Comprehending." *The Reading Teacher* 62 (6): 512–21.

Avalos, M., A. Plasencia, C. Chavez, and J. Rascón. 2007. "Modified Guided Reading: Gateway to English as a Second Language and Literacy Learning." *The Reading Teacher* 61 (4): 318–29.

Beck, I., M. McKeown, R. Hamilton, and L. Kucan. 1997. *Questioning the Author.* Newark, DE: International Reading Association.

Bennett-Armistead, S., N. Duke, and A. Moses. 2005. *Literacy and the Youngest Learner: Best Practices for Educators of Children from Birth to 5.* Scholastic: New York.

Blachman, B. 2000. "Phonological Awareness." In *Handbook of Reading Research, Volume 3,* ed. M. Kamil, P. Mosenthal, P. Pearson, and R. Barr, 483–502. Mahwah, NJ: Erlbaum.

Bomer, R. 1998. "Transactional Heat and Light: More Explicit Literacy Learning." *Language Arts* 76 (1): 11–18.

Braunger, J., and J. Lewis. 2006. *Building a Knowledge Base in Reading.* Newark, DE, and Urbana, IL: IRA/NCTE.

Caldwell, J. 2002. *Reading Assessment: A Primer for Teachers and Tutors.* New York: Guilford.

Caldwell, J., and L. Leslie. 2009. *Intervention Strategies to Follow Informal Reading Inventory Assessment: So What Do I Do Now?* 2d ed. Boston: Pearson.

Calhoon, J., and L. Leslie. 2002. "A Longitudinal Study of the Effects of Word Frequency and Rime-Neighborhood Size on Beginning Readers' Rime Reading Accuracy in Words and Nonwords." *Journal of Literacy Research* 34 (1): 39–58.

Calkins, L. 2001. *The Art of Teaching Reading*. New York. Longman.

Cappellini, M. 2005. *Balancing Reading and Language Learning: A Resource for Teaching English Language Learners, K–5*. Portland, ME: Stenhouse.

Chinn, C., and R. Anderson. 1998. "The Structure of Discussions That Promote Reasoning." *Teachers College Record* 100 (2): 315–68.

Christensen, L. 2001. "Where I'm From: Inviting Students' Lives into the Classroom." In *Rethinking Our Classrooms: Teaching for Equity and Justice, Volume 2*, ed. B. Bigelow, B. Harvey, S. Karp, and L. Miller, 6–10. Williston, VT: Rethinking Schools.

Clay, M. 1991. *Becoming Literate: The Construction of Inner Control*. Portsmouth, NH: Heinemann.

Dudley-Marling, C., and P. Paugh. 2004. *A Classroom Teacher's Guide to Struggling Readers*. Portsmouth, NH: Heinemann.

Ehri, L. 1998. "Grapheme-Phoneme Knowledge Is Essential for Learning to Read Words in English." In *Word Recognition in Beginning Literacy*, ed. J. Metsala and L. Ehri, 3–40. Mahwah, NJ: Erlbaum.

Einstein, A. 2008. "Unpublished Opening Lecture for the Course on the Theory of Relativity in Argentina, 1925." *Science in Context* 21 (3): 451–59.

Ferguson, A., E. Harding, K. Helmer, and S. Suh. 2003. "Miscue Analysis of Native and Non-Native Speakers." *Arizona Working Papers in Second Language Acquisition and Teaching* 10: 51–67.

Flurkey, A. 2006. "What's 'Normal' About Real Reading?" In *The Truth About DIBELS*, ed. K. Goodman, 40–49. Portsmouth, NH: Heinemann.

Fountas, I., and G. S. Pinnell. 2006. *Leveled Books: Matching Texts to Readers for Effective Teaching*. Portsmouth, NH: Heinemann.

———. 2008. *Benchmark Assessment System*. Portsmouth, NH: Heinemann.

Freire, P. 1970. *The Pedagogy of the Oppressed*. New York: Seabury.

Fry, E. 1997. *1000 Instant Words: The Most Common Words for Teaching Reading, Writing, and Spelling*. Chicago, IL: NTC/Contemporary.

Gee, J. 1999. "Critical Issues: Reading and the New Literacy Studies: Reframing the National Academy of Sciences Report on Reading." *Journal of Literacy Research* 31 (3): 355–74.

German, D., and R. Newman. 2007. "Oral Reading Skills of Children with Oral Language (Word Finding Difficulties)." *Reading Psychology* 28 (5): 397–442.

Gersten, R., D. Compton, C. Connor, J. Dimino, L. Santoro, S. Linan-Thompson, and W. Tilly. 2008. "Assisting Students Struggling with Reading: Response to Intervention (RtI) and Multi-Tier Intervention in the Primary Grades: A Practice Guide" (NCEE 2009 40-45). Washington, DC: National Center for Education Evaluation and Regional Assistance, Institute of Education Sciences, US Department of Education. Available at http://ies.ed.gov/ncee/wwc/publications/practiceguides/.

Goodman, K. 1996. *On Reading*. Portsmouth, NH: Heinemann.

———. 2006. "A Critical Review of DIBELS." In *The Truth About DIBELS*, ed. K. Goodman, 1–39. Portsmouth, NH: Heinemann.

Goodman, Y. 1996a. "Kidwatching: Observing Children in the Classroom." In *Notes from a Kidwatcher: Selected Writings of Yetta M. Goodman*, ed. S. Wilde, 219–27. Portsmouth, NH: Heinemann.

———. 1996b. "Respect for the Language Learner." In *Notes from a Kidwatcher: Selected Writings of Yetta M. Goodman*, ed. S. Wilde, 247–51. Portsmouth, NH: Heinemann.

Goodman, Y., and A. Marek. 1996. *Retrospective Miscue Analysis*. Katohah, NY: Richard C. Owen.

Goodman, Y., D. Watson, and C. Burke. 2005. *Reading Strategies: Focus on Comprehension*. 2d ed. Katohah, NY: Richard C. Owen.

González, N. 2005. "Beyond Culture: The Hybridity of Funds of Knowledge." In *Funds of Knowledge*, ed. N. González, L. Moll, and C. Amanti, 29–46. Mahwah, NJ: Erlbaum.

Guthrie, J., and A. Wigfield. 2000. "Engagement and Motivation in Reading." In *Handbook of Reading Research*, Vol. 3, ed. M. Kamil, P. Mosenthal, P. Pearson, and R. Barr, 403–22. New York: Erlbaum.

Hadaway, N., S. Vardell, and T. Young. 2004. *What Every Teacher Should Know About English Language Learners*. Boston: Allyn and Bacon.

Hall, S. 2008. *Implementing Response to Invention*. Thousand Oaks, CA: Corwin.

Hasbrouck, J., and C. Inhot. 2009. "Curriculum-Based Measurement: From Skeptic to Advocate." RTI Action Network. Available at www.rtinetwork.org/Essential/Assessment/Progress/ar/CBMAdvocate/1.

Hasbrouck, J., and G. Tindal. 2006. "Oral Reading Fluency Norms: A Valuable Assessment Tool for Reading Teachers." *The Reading Teacher* 59 (7): 636–44.

Howard, M. 2009. *RTI from All Sides*. Portsmouth, NH: Heinemann.

Keene, E., and R. Zimmermann. 2007. *Mosaic of Thought: Teaching Comprehension in a Reader's Workshop*. 2d ed. Portsmouth, NH: Heinemann.

Kovaleski, J. 2009. "The Critical Components of RTI." CEC's RTI Blog. Available at http://cecblog.typepad.com/rti/2009/05/the-critical-components-of-rti.html.

LaBerge, D., and S. Samuels. 1974. "Toward a Theory of Automatic Information Processing in Reading." *Cognitive Psychology* 6 (2): 293–323.

Lenz, K. 2006. "Creating School-Wide Conditions for High-Quality Learning Strategy Classroom Instruction." *Intervention in School and Clinic* 41 (5): 261–66.

Leslie, L., and J. Caldwell. 2005. *Qualitative Reading Inventory-4*. 4th ed. Boston: Allyn and Bacon.

Manning, M., S. Chumley, and C. Underbakke. 2006. *Scientific Reading Assessment: Targeted Intervention and Follow-Up Lessons*. Portsmouth, NH: Heinemann.

Manyak, P. 2008. "Phonemes in Use: Multiple Activities for a Critical Process." *The Reading Teacher* 6 (18): 659–62.

Manzo, A. 1969. "The ReQuest Procedure." *Journal of Reading* 13: 123–26.

McCarthy, P. 2008/2009. "Using Sound Boxes Systematically to Develop Phonemic Awareness." *The Reading Teacher* 62 (4): 346–49.

McKenna, M., and R. Robinson. 2002. *Teaching Through Text: Reading and Writing in the Content Areas*. Boston: Allyn and Bacon.

McTigue, E., E. Washburn, and J. Liew. 2009. "Academic Resilience and Reading: Building Successful Readers." *The Reading Teacher* 62 (5): 422–32.

Meier, D. 2004. *The Young Child's Memory for Words: Developing First and Second Language and Literacy*. New York: Teachers College Press.

Mesmer, H., and S. Cuming. 2009. "Text-Reader Matching: Matching the Needs of Struggling Readers." In *Finding the Right Texts: What Works for Beginning and Struggling Readers*, ed. E. Hiebert and M. Sailors, 149–76. New York: Guilford.

Mesmer, E., and H. Mesmer. 2008. "Response to Intervention (RTI): What Teachers of Reading Need to Know." *The Reading Teacher* 62 (4): 280–90.

Moll, L., and J. Greenberg. 1990. "Creating Zones of Possibilities: Combining Social Contexts for Instruction." In *Vygotsky and Education*, ed. L. Moll, 319–48. Cambridge, UK: Cambridge University Press.

Nathan, R., and K. Stanovich. 1991. "The Causes and Consequences of Differences in Reading Fluency." *Theory into Practice* 30: 176–84.

National Association of State Directors of Special Education (NASDSE). 2006. "Response to Intervention: NASDSE and CASE White Paper on RTI." Available at www.nasdse.org/Portals/0/Documents/Download%20Publications/ RtIAnAdministratorsPerspective1-06.pdf.

National Center on Response to Intervention. 2009. Available at www .rti4success.org.

National Reading Panel. 2000. *Teaching Children to Read: An Evidenced-Based Assessment of the Scientific Research Literature on Reading and Its Implications for Reading Instruction.* Washington, DC: National Institute of Child Health and Human Development.

O'Connor, C., F. Morrison, B. Fishman, and C. Ponitz. 2009. "The ISI Classroom Observation System: Examining the Literacy Instruction Provided to Individual Students." *Educational Researcher* 38 (2): 85–100.

Palincsar, A. 1986. "Reciprocal Teaching." In *Teaching Reading as Thinking*. Oak Brook, IL: North Central Regional Educational Laboratory.

Palincsar, A., and A. Brown. 1985. "Reciprocal Teaching: Activities to Promote Read(ing) with Your Mind." In *Reading, Thinking, and Concept Development: Strategies for the Classroom*, ed. T. Harris and E. Cooper, 147–58. New York: The College Board.

Pearson, D. 2006. Foreword to *The Truth About DIBELS*, ed. K. Goodman, v–xxiv. Portsmouth, NH: Heinemann.

Peterson, R., and M. Eeds. 1990. *Grand Conversations: Literature Groups in Action.* New York: Scholastic.

Powell, D., and R. Aram. 2008. "Spelling in Parts: A Strategy for Spelling and Decoding Polysyllabic Words." *The Reading Teacher* 61 (7): 567–70.

Pressley, M., R. Allington, R. Wharton-McDonald, C. Block, and L. Morrow. 2001. *Learning to Read: Lessons from Exemplary First-Grade Classrooms.* New York: Guilford.

Rasinski, T. 2004. "Creating Fluent Readers." *Educational Leadership* 61 (6): 46–51.

Rasinski, T., N. Padak, W. Linek, and E. Sturtevant. 1994. "Effects of Fluency Development on Urban Second-Grade Readers." *Journal of Educational Research* 87: 158–65.

Rea, D., and S. Mercuri. 2006. *Research-Based Strategies for English Language Learners.* Portsmouth, NH: Heinemann.

Rosenshine, B., and C. Meister. 1994. "Reciprocal Teaching: A Review of the Research." *Review of Educational Research* 64 (4): 479–530.

RTI Action Network. 2009. Available at www.rtinetwork.org.

Samuels, S. 2002. "The Method of Repeated Readings." In *Evidence-Based Reading Instruction: Putting the National Reading Panel Report into Practice*, 85–91. Newark, DE: International Reading Association.

Shanahan, T. 2008. "Implications of RTI for the Reading Teacher." In *Response to Intervention: A Framework for Reading Educators*, ed. D. Fuchs, L. Fuchs, and S. Vaughn, 105–22. Newark, DE: International Reading Association.

Stanovich, K. 1986. "Matthew Effects in Reading: Some Consequences of Individual Differences in the Acquisition of Literacy." *Reading Research Quarterly* 21: 360–407.

Tierney, R., and C. Thome. 2006. "Is DIBELS Leading Us Down the Wrong Path?" In *The Truth About DIBELS*, ed. K. Goodman, 50–59. Portsmouth, NH: Heinemann.

Valencia, S., and M. Buly. 2005. "Behind Test Scores: What Struggling Readers Really Need." In *Reading Assessment: Principles and Practices for Elementary Teachers*, 2d ed., ed. S. Barrentine and S. Stokes, 134–46. Newark, DE: International Reading Association.

Villaume, S., and E. Brabham. 2002. "Comprehension Instruction: Beyond Strategies." *The Reading Teacher* 55 (7): 672–75.

Vygotsky, L. 1978. *Mind in Society: The Development of Higher Psychological Processes*, ed. M. Cole, V. John-Steiner, S. Scribner, and E. Souberman. Cambridge, MA: Harvard University Press.

Wade, S., and E. Moje. 2001. "The Role of Text in Classroom Learning: Beginning an Online Dialogue." *Reading Online* 5 (4). Available at www.readingonline.org/articles/art_index.asp?HREF=/articles/handbook/wade/index.html.

Walczyk, J. 2000. "The Interplay Between Automatic and Control Processes in Reading." *Reading Research Quarterly* 35 (4): 554–66.

What Works Clearinghouse. 2009. "Best Practice for RTI: Intensive, Systematic Instruction for Some Students." Available at www.readingrockets.org/article/30673.

White, T., J. Sowell, and A. Yanagihara. 1989. "Teaching Elementary Students to Use Word-Part Clues." *The Reading Teacher* 42: 302–309.

White, Z. 2008. *Playing with Poems: Word Study Lessons for Shared Reading, K–2*. Portsmouth, NH: Heinemann.

Whitmore, K., P. Martens, Y. Goodman, and G. Owocki. 2004. "Critical Lessons from the Transactional Perspective on Early Literacy Research." *Journal of Early Childhood Literacy* 4 (3): 291–325.

Woods, M., and A. Moe. 2007. *Analytical Reading Inventory*. 8th ed. Upper Saddle River, NJ: Pearson.

Wylie, R., and D. Durrell. 1970. "Teaching Vowels Through Phonograms." *Elementary English* 47: 787–91.

Yopp, H. 1992. "Developing Phonemic Awareness in Young Children." *The Reading Teacher* 49: 20–29.

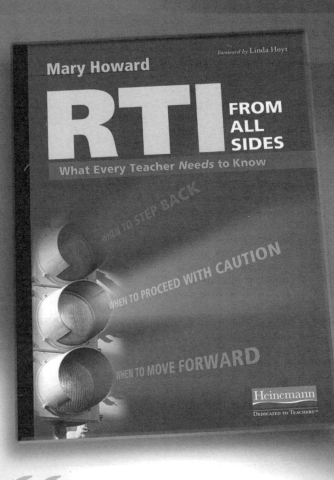